John W Dudmun

The Masonic Choir

A collection of hymns and tunes

John W Dudmun

The Masonic Choir
A collection of hymns and tunes

ISBN/EAN: 9783337298173

Printed in Europe, USA, Canada, Australia, Japan

Cover: Foto ©Thomas Meinert / pixelio.de

More available books at **www.hansebooks.com**

THE

MASONIC CHOIR:

A

COLLECTION OF HYMNS AND TUNES,

ORIGINAL AND SELECTED,

FOR THE USE OF THE FRATERNITY.

BY SIR KNIGHT JOHN W. DADMUN.

ARRANGED FOR MALE VOICES

By Bro. O. B. BROWN.

BOSTON:

Published by G. D. Russell & Company, 126 Tremont Street.

Entered according to Act of Congress, in the year 1864, by
G. D. RUSSELL AND COMPANY AND J. W. DADMUN,
In the Clerk's Office of the District Court, for the District of Massachusetts.

G. D. Russell & Company, Music Printers and Stereotypers, 126 Tremont Street, Boston.

THE MASONIC CHOIR.

PART I. BLUE LODGE.

OPENING HYMN.

[LISBON. S. M.]

I. READ.

1. Kind Fa - ther! hear our prayer,— We bow be - fore thy throne;

2. With - in these walls may Peace And Har - mo - ny be found;

O may we find ac- cept-ance there, And peace be - fore un - known.

May Faith and Char - i - ty increase, And Hope and Love a - bound.

OPENING HYMN.

[CORONATION. C. M.]

O. HOLDEN.

1ST TENOR.

1. When met in Friendship's sa - cred name, We round an al - tar stand,

2D TENOR.

2. Here let our heart-felt prayers u - nite For him who comes in love,
3. In cheerful hour, or saddening day, When memory brings its tear,

1ST BASS.

4. Thus fond-ly known the joys of time That brothers kind - ly prove,

2D BASS.

Then each shall own re - li - gion's claim, And bow at her com - mand,

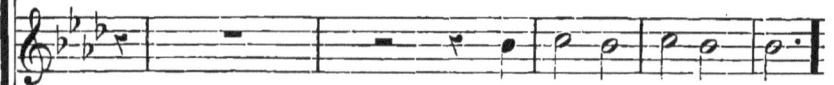

Each brother blest in that pure light Re - flect - ed from a - bove,
Though friends we love are far a - way, We'll think of kind - ness here,

Our hopes shall point to that fair clime, Where dwells Im - MOR - TAL LOVE,

When each shall own Re - li - gion's claim, And bow at her command.

Each brother blest in that pure light Re - flect - ed from a - bove.
Though friends we love are far a - way, We'll think of kind - ness here.

Our hopes shall point to that dear clime, Where dwells IM - MOR - TAL LOVE.

3.   OPENING HYMN. C. M.

1 Great Architect of Earth and Heaven,
  By time nor space confined,
Enlarge our love to comprehend
  Our brethren, all mankind,

2 Where'er we are, whate'er we do,
  Thy presence let us own;
Thine Eye, all-seeing, marks our deeds,
  To Thee all thoughts are known.

3 While nature's works and science' laws,
  We labor to reveal,
O! be our duty done to Thee,
  With fervency and zeal.

4 With Faith our guide, and humble Hope.
  Warm Charity and Love,
May all at last be raised to share
  Thy perfect light above.

4.   CLOSING HYMN. C. M.

1 Now we must close our labors here
  Though sad it is to part;
May Love, Relief, and Truth sincere,
  Unite each brother's heart.

2 Now to our homes let's haste away,
  Still filled with love and light;
And may each heart, in kindness, say
  Good night, brother, good night.

5.   CLOSING HYMN. C. M.

1 Sweet as the dew on herb and flower,
  That silently distils,
At evening's soft and balmy hour,
  On Zion's fruitful hills.

2 So, with mild influence from above,
  Shall promised grace descend;
Till universal peace and love
  O'er all the earth extend.

CLOSING HYMN.

[AULD LANG SYNE. C. M.]

1ST TENOR.

1. Should auld ac-quaint-ance be for-got, And nev - er brought to mind,

2D TENOR.

1ST BASS.

2. Then here's a hand, my trus - ty frien', And gie's a hand o' thine,

2D BASS.

Should auld ac-quaint-ance be for-got, And days of auld lang syne.

We'll take a right gude wil - lie waught, For auld, for auld lang syne.

7. OPENING HYMN. C. M.

1 Come, brothers of the mystic tie,
  Our social work begun,—
We'll raise an opening song on high
  To HIM, the ONLY ONE!
With hearts united, firm and free,
  We round our altar stand;

Who best can work, and best agree,
Are dearest in our band.

2 Come, kindle, at our holy fire,
  Fraternal thoughts and kind;
Each worthy act and pure desire
  Shall kindred wishes bind.
With hearts united, firm and free, &c.

For auld lang syne, my dear, For auld lang syne, We'll

For auld lang syne, my dear, For auld lang syne, We'll

take a cup of kind-ness yet, For auld lang syne.

take a cup of kind-ness yet, For auld lang syne.

8. CLOSING HYMN. C. M.

1 We meet in love, we part in peace,
Our council labors o'er;
We'll ask, e'er life's best days shall cease,
To meet in time once more,
Cho.—'Mid fairest scenes to memory dear,
In change of joy and pain;
We'll think of friends assembled here,
And hope to meet again.

2 Though changes mark time's onward way
In all we fondly claim,

Fraternal hopes shall ne'er decay—
Our landmarks still the same.—Cho.

3 Our Faith unmoved, with Truth our guide,
As seasons mark our clime;
Through winter's chill, or summer's pride,
We'll hail the Art Sublime.—Cho.

4 When life shall find its silent close,
With Hope's kind promise blest;
In that Grand Lodge may all repose,
Where joys immortal rest.—Cho.

OPENING HYMN.

[DUKE STREET. L. M.]

1st Tenor.

1. The spacious world by Wisdom planned, And spread beneath the star - ry skies;

2d Tenor.

2. Our Great Grand Master gave it birth; He squared and laid its cor - ner stone;

1st Bass.

3. He formed yon broad ex - pan - sive skies, And round the verge of that blue dome,

2d Bass.

Was made a Tem-ple strong and grand, From which a Mason's prayer should rise.

His strength and Wisdom spread this earth, At his com - mand the work was done.

In pomp transcendent spread those skies, Arched the broad heavens, the Mason's home.

4 While in our Lodge, with songs divine,
By faith our prayers ascend to heaven;
Strength, Wisdom, Beauty, all combine,
And Faith and Hope and Love are given.

5 Then when our works are found complete,
And all Masonic graces blend;
May we, with all good Masons meet,
Where all life's toils and cares shall end.

10 OPENING HYMN. L. M.

1 From East to West, o'er land and sea,
Where brothers meet and friends agree,
Let incense rise from hearts sincere,
The dearest offering gathered here.

2 Let notes of praise united tell
Of thoughts most kind where brothers dwell;
Though clouds may dim our darkened way,
Some kindly hand shall be our stay.

3 Our trust reposed on HIM alone
Who ne'er will contrite hearts disown,
Our Faith shall mark that Holy Light
Whose beams our dearest joys unite.

11 OPENING HYMN. L. M.

1 How dear the place where brothers true
Their holy pledge of Faith renew!
Let notes of love responsive rise—
From East to West—to farthest skies.

2 While here sweet Hope its presence bears,
No fear indulged, no anxious cares,
Let notes of love responsive rise—
From East to West—to farthest skies.

3 May gentle Charity here find
United friends and brothers kind;
Let notes of Love responsive rise—
From East to West—to farthest skies.

4 To HIM, our MASTER, throned in light,
Let every voice in praise unite;
Let notes of Love responsive rise—
From East to West—to farthest skies.

12 CLOSING. L. M.

Eternal are thy mercies, Lord;
Eternal truth attends thy Word;
Thy praise shall sound from shore to shore,
Till suns shall rise and set no more.

13 INITIATION. L. M.

1 While journeying on our homeward way,
By love fraternal gently led,
SUPREME CONDUCTOR! THEE we pray
To smooth the dangerous path we tread.

2 No fear shall cross the trusting heart,
Our faith reposed on HIM above;
No dearer joy can life impart
Than gently breathes in words of love.

3 When earthly ties shall fade and die,
When earthly joys shall come no more,
SUPREME CONDUCTOR! then supply
Thy holy aid, when time is o'er.

14 INITIATION. L. M.

1 Far from the world's cold strife and pride,
Come join our peaceful, happy band;
Come, stranger, we your feet will guide
Where truth and love shall hold command.

2 Although in untried paths you tread,
And filled, perhaps, with anxious fear;
A brother's faithful hand shall lead
Where doubt and darkness disappear.

3 Here may you in our labors join,
And prove yourself a brother true;
All sordid, selfish cares resign,
And keep our sacred truths in view.

15 INITIATION. L. M.

1 Dangers of every form attend
Your steps, as onward you proceed;
No earthly power can now befriend
Or aid you in this time of need.

2 Confide your trust in him alone
Who rules all things above, below;
Send your petitions to his throne,
For he alone can help you now.

OPENING HYMN.

[ORTONVILLE. C.M.]

1ST TENOR.

1. Lo! what an en-ter-tain-ing sight Are brethren who a - gree; Brethren, whose cheerful

2D TENOR.

2. 'Tis like the oil, di - vine-ly sweet, On Aaron's reverend head; The trickling drops per-

1ST BASS.

3. 'Tis pleasant as the morning dews, That fall on Zion's hill; Where God his mildest

2D BASS.

hearts u - nite In bonds of pu - ri - ty, In bonds of pu - ri - ty.

fumed his feet, And o'er his garments spread, And o'er his garments spread.

glo - ry shows, And makes his grace dis - til, And makes his grace dis - til.

MASTER MASON.

1 Teach me the measure of my days,
 Thou maker of my frame;
I would survey life's narrow space,
 And learn how frail I am.

2 A span is all that we can boast,
{ How short the fleeting time!
Man is but vanity and dust,
 In all his flower and prime.

MASTER MASON. (OPENING.)

1 Come, Masters of the Art, unite,
 And may this meeting prove,
To all th' assembled sons of light,
 A strengthened bond of love.

2 May Friendship and Morality,
 With true fraternal love,
Be found in every Mason's heart,
 And all his actions move.

[ST THOMAS. S. M.]

1ST TENOR.

1. Great source of light and love, To thee our songs we raise! Oh,

2D TENOR.

2. May this fra - ter - nal band, In Faith and Hope be blessed; In

1ST BASS.

3. May all the sons of peace, Their ev' - ry grace im - prove, Till

in the tem - ple, Lord, a - bove, Hear and ac - cept our praise!

Char - i - ty thrice bless - ed stand, In pu - ri - ty be dressed.

dis - cord through the na - tions cease, And all the world be love.

CLOSING HYMN. S. M.

1. Now, brothers, we must part,
   Where we have met in peace;
   Where harmony its joys impart,
   And strife and discord cease.

2 We on the Level meet,
   Upon the Square we part;

May truth, and love, and friendship sweet,
Pervade each brother's heart.

3 Here, Lord, before we part,
   Help us to bless thy name;
   Let every tongue, and every heart,
   Praise and adore the same.

[TAPPAN, 8s & 6s.]   G. KINGSLEY.

1ST TENOR.

1. This world's not all a fleeting show, For man's il - lu - sion given; He that hath

2D TENOR.

2. And he that walks life's thorny way, With feelings calm and even,—Whose path is

1ST BASS.

3. He that the Christian's course has run, And all his foes forgiven, Who measures

2D BASS.

soothed a widow's woe, Or wiped an orphan's tear, doth know There's something here of heaven.

lit from day to day By virtue's bright and steady ray, Hath something felt of heaven.

out life's little span In love to God and love to man, On earth has tast - ed heaven.

OPENING HYMN. 8s & 6s.

1 Blest is the hour when cares depart,
  And earthly scenes are far!
When tears of woe forget to start,
And gently dawns upon the heart
  Devotion's holy star.

2 Blest is the place, when Brothers bend,
  And fervent prayers arise;
Where kindred hearts in union blend,
And all the soul's affections tend
  Beyond the veiling skies.

[BALERMA. C. M.]

1ST TENOR.

1. Al - might - y   Fa - ther! God of Love! Be - hold thy   serv - ant here!

2D TENOR.

1ST BASS.

2. Tho' darksome skies shall o'er him lower, And   dangers   fill   the way;

2D BASS.

O, may   he   trust in Thee   above,   Free thou his   heart from fear.

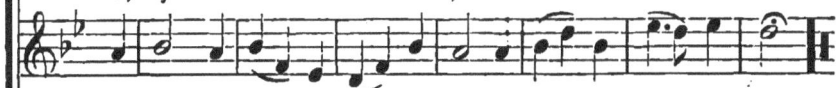

Support   him with   thy gra - cious power, And be   his   con - stant stay.

FELLOW CRAFT. [BALERMA. C. M.]

1. O, welcome, brother, to our band;
Here Truth and Friendship reign,
And Love and Virtue, hand in hand,
Their bonds of peace maintain.

2. O welcome—if thy heart be true,
Thou'lt find with us a home;

We're daily adding columns new
Unto our glorious dome.

3. Now let our heartfelt prayers arise,
For blessings on his brow,
And bear our offering to the skies,
For him who joins us now.

FELLOW CRAFT.

[LYONS 10s & 11s.]

HAYDN.

1st Tenor.

2d Tenor.

1. Come, Craftsmen, assembled our pleasure to share, Who walk by the Plumb, and who work by the [Square;

1st Bass.

2d Bass.

While traveling in love, on the Level of time, Sweet Hope shall light on to a far better clime.

2 We'll seek in our labors the Spirit Divine,
Our temple to bless, and our hearts to refine ;
And thus to our altar a tribute we'll bring,
While, joined in true Friendship, our anthem we sing.

3 See Order and Beauty rise gently to view,
Each brother a column, so perfect and true ?
When Order shall cease, and when temples decay,
May each fairer columns immortal survey.

[ZEPHYR. L. M.]   WM. B. BRADBURY.

1ST TENOR.

1. Great God! wilt thou meet with us here, And bless us in our works of love?

2D TENOR.

2. May each be found a liv-ing stone, For heavenly mansions tried and squared;

1ST BASS.

3. By the strong grip of Ju-dah's king, May we be raised to realms of peace;

2D BASS.

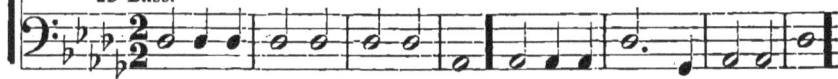

Thy sa-cred name we all re-vere, Oh! grant us blessings from a-bove.

When all our earth-ly sands are run, The scythe of time find us prepared.

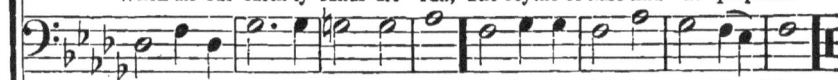

There constant songs of prais-es sing, In that Grand Lodge of end-less bliss.

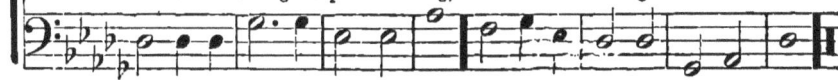

---

28   MASTER MASON. L. M.

1 Blest is the man who stands in awe
Of God, and loves his sacred law ;
His seed on earth shall be renowned,
And with successive honors crowned.

2 Beset with threat'ning dangers round,
Unmoved shall he maintain his ground ;
The sweet remembrance of the just
Shall flourish, when he sleeps in dust.

29   MASTER MASON. L. M.

1 Death, like an ever-flowing stream,
Sweeps us away—our life's a dream—
An empty tale—a morning flower—
Cut down and withered in an hour.

2 Teach us, O Lord, how frail is man ;
And kindly lengthen out our span,
Till, cleansed by grace, we all may be
Prepared to die, and dwell with thee.

CONSTITUTING A LODGE.

[UXBRIDGE. L. M.]

L. MASON.

1ST TENOR.

1. Let us re - mem-ber, in our youth, Be - fore the e - vil days draw 'nigh,

2D TENOR.

2. Or sun, or moon, or plan - et's light Grow dark, or clouds re - turn in gloom;

1ST BASS.

3. Let us in youth re - mem - ber Him Who formed our frame and spir - it gave,

2D BASS.

Our GREAT CRE-A - TOR, and his TRUTH, Ere memory fail, and plea-sure fly;

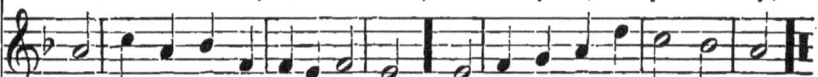

Ere vi - tal spark no more in - cite; When strength shall bow, and years consume.

Ere windows of the mind grow dim, Or door of speech ob - struct-ed wave.

4 When voice of bird fresh terrors wake,
  And music's daughters charm no more;
Or fear to rise, with trembling shake,
  Along the path we travel o'er.

5 In youth, to God let memory cling,
  Before desire shall fail or wane,

Or e'er be loosed life's silver string,
  Or bowl at fountain rent in twain.

6 For man to his long home doth go,
  And mourners group around his urn;
Our dust to dust again must flow,
  And spirits unto God return.

[HEBRON. L. M.]

L. MASON.

1st TENOR.

1. Had I the tongues of Greek and Jews, And no-bler speech than an-gels use,

2d TENOR.

2. Were I in-spired to preach, and tell All that is done in heaven and hell,
3. Should I dis-tri-bute all my store, To feed the crav-ings of the poor;

1st BASS.

4. If love to God and love to men Be ab-sent, all my hopes are vain:

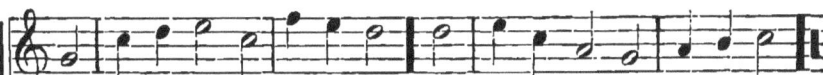

2d BASS.

If love be ab-sent, I am found, Like tinkling brass, an emp-ty sound.

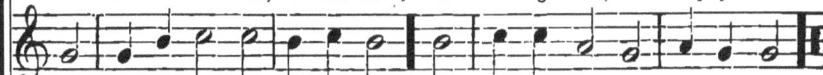

Or could my faith the world re-move, Still I am noth-ing without love.
Or give my bo-dy to the flame, To gain a mar-tyr's glorious name;

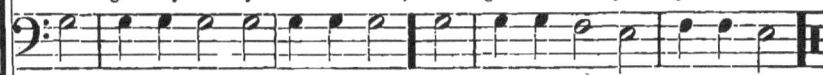

Nor tongues, nor gifts, nor fie-ry zeal, The work of love can e'er ful-fill.

32. OPENING OR CLOSING.

1 How blest the sacred tie, that binds
In sweet communion kindred minds!
How sweet the heavenly course they run,
Whose hearts, whose faith, whose hopes are one.

2 Together oft they seek the place
Where Masons meet with smiling face;

How high, how strong their raptures swell,
There's none but kindred souls can tell.

3 Nor shall the glowing flame expire,
When dimly burns frail nature's fire;
Then shall they meet in realms above,
A heaven of joy, a heaven of love.

CONSTITUTING A LODGE.

[LAKE ENON. S. M.]

1. Come, bro-thers, join each voice, With kind-ly thoughts sin-cere ;

2. Ne'er o'er our calm re-treat Let notes of dis-cord roll;
3. Though years on years shall come, Though chang-es mark our skies,

4. May peace for-ev-er find Its calm re-spons-es here,

Here bid the suf-fering heart re-joice, And dry af-flic-tion's tear.

But songs of joy, in ac-cents sweet, Our dear-est thoughts con-trol.
Here be a bro-ther's wel-come home, Where gen-tle Hope re-lies.

While friendship's pledge shall be enshrined In ho-ly bonds sin-cere.

34 DEDICATION OR CONSECRATION.

1 Great source of light and love,
  To Thee our songs we raise!
O! in thy temple, Lord, above,
  Hear and accept our praise!

2 Shine on this festive day,
  Succeed its hoped design,
And may our Charity display
  A love resembling thine.

3 May this fraternal band,
  Now { Consecrated } —blest,
      { Dedicated }
In Union all distinguished stand,
  In Purity be drest.

4 May all the sons of peace
  Their every grace improve,
Till discord through the nation cease,
  And all the world be love.

CONSTITUTING A LODGE.

[SILVER STREET. S. M.]   I. SMITH.

1ST TENOR.

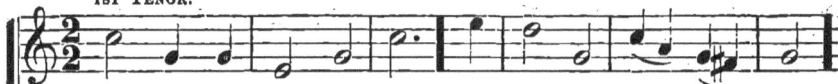

1. Be - hold, how good it is, And what a joy to see,

2D TENOR.

2. 'T is like the pre - cious oil They poured on Aa - ron's head,
3. Or as re - fresh - ing dew On Her - mon's mount dis - tils;

1ST BASS.

4. For there the Lord com - mands, And doth his bless - ing give,—

2D BASS.

When brethren with each oth - er dwell In love and u - ni - ty.

Which down his hair and gar - ment flowed, And fra - grant o - dors spread.
Or like the pearl - y drops that shine On Zi - on's joy - ful hills.

The fore - taste of that bless - ed - ness Which shall for - ev - er live.

---

36   CLOSING.   S. M.

1 Now, brothers, we must part,
    Where we have met in peace,
Where harmony its joys impart,
    And strife and discord cease.

2 We on the Level meet,
    Upon the Square we part;

May Truth and Love, and Friendship sweet,
    Pervade each brother's heart.

3 Here, Lord, before we part,
    Help us to bless thy name;
Let every tongue, and every heart,
    Praise and adore the same.

[WARE. L. M.]

G. KINGSLEY.

1ST TENOR.

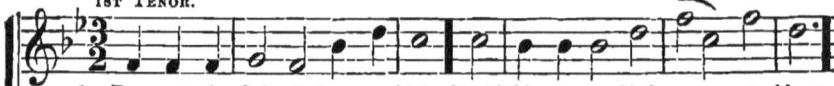

1. Pour out thy Spir - it from on high; Lord! thine as-sem-bled serv - ants bless;

2D TENOR.

2. With - in this tem-ple, where we stand To teach the truth as taught by Thee,
3. Fer - vor and Zeal free - ly im - part; Firmness, with meekness from a - bove,

1ST BASS.

4. And when our work is finished here, May we in Hope our charge re - sign:

2D BASS.

Graces and gifts to each sup - ply, And clothe us with thy right - eous-ness.

In fa - vor bless this cho-sen band, With Wisdom, Strength and U - ni - ty.
That each may with a faithful heart Here la - bor for the cause of Love.

When thou, Grand Master, shalt appear, May we and all man - kind be thine.

38. DEDICATION. CLOSING. L. M.

1 Great Architect of heaven and earth,
To whom all nature owes its birth;
Thou spoke! and vast creation stood,
Surveyed the work—pronounced it good.

2 Lord, can'st thou deign to own and bless
This humble dome, this sacred place?
Oh! let thy spirit's presence shine
Within these walls—this house of thine.

3 'T was reared in honor of thy name;
Here kindle, Lord, the sacred flame:
Oh! make it burn in every heart,
And never from this place depart.

4 Lord, here the wants of all supply,
And fit our souls to dwell on high;
From service in this humble place,
Raise us to praise thee face to face.

[MISSIONARY CHANT. L. M.]

1st TENOR.   CH. ZEUNER.

1. All hon-ors to our MASTER pay, Who bade our ho-ly tem-ple rise;

2D TENOR.

2. We hail our ho-ly Patron's name, Whose bright ex-am-ple guides us still;

1ST BASS.

3. While thus we seek, in pure de-sire, Im-mor-tal bliss in realms a-bove,

2D BASS.

While here we jour-ney on our way Our thanks shall reach to far-thest skies.

[To Freemasonry.]

His high-est hon-ors we pro-claim, While grateful thanks our tem-ple fill.

[To Virtue.]

Our hearts shall kin-dle at the fire Whose light is U-ni-ver-sal Love.

[To Universal Benevolence.]

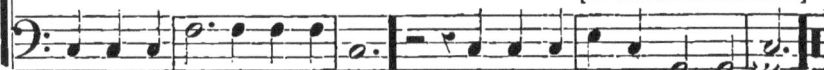

40. DEDICATION. L. M.

1 Genius of Masonry, descend,
  And with thee bring thy spotless train ;
Constant our sacred rites attend,
  While we adore thy peaceful reign.

    [To Freemasonry.]

2 Bring with thee Virtue, brightest maid ;
  Bring Love, bring Truth and Friendship here,
While kind Relief will lend her aid,
  To smooth the wrinkled brow of care.

    [To Virtue.]

3 Come Charity, with goodness crowned,
  Encircled in thy heavenly robe,
Diffuse thy blessings all around,
  To every corner of the globe.

    [To Universal Benevolence.]

4 To Heaven's high Architect all praise,
  All praise, all gratitude be given,
Who deigned the human soul to raise,
  By mystic secrets sprung from heaven.

DEDICATION.

[ITALIAN HYMN. 6s & 4s.]   GIARDINI.

1ST TENOR.

1. Thou! who art God a-lone, Accept be - fore thy throne Our fervent prayer! To fill with

2D TENOR.

2. As through the u - ni-verse All nature's works di-verse, Thy praise accord ; Let Faith up-

1ST BASS.

3. Spirit of Truth and Love, Descending from a - bove, Our hearts inflame, Till Mason-

2D BASS.

light and grace This house, thy dwelling-place, And bless thy chosen race, O God, draw near.

on us shine, And Chari - ty combine, With Hope, to make us thine, Je-ho-vah, Lord.

ry's control Shall build in∙one the whole, A Temple of the soul To thy great name.

42 ANNIVERSARY HYMN. 6s & 4s.

1 E'er this vast world was made,
Or its foundation laid,
  Our Art begun ;
Cherub and Cherubim,
Seraph and Seraphim,
Joined in one glorious hymn,
  Before the throne.

2 God their Grand Master was ;
Fixed their unerring laws ;
  By his decree ;

Faith, Hope, and Charity,
Friendship and Unity,
Truth, Love, and Secrecy,
  All laws divine.

3 Oh may our constant theme,
To Heaven's Great King, Supreme !
  Be grateful Love :
May we whene'er we meet,   ⎫
Chant Hallelujahs sweet,   ⎬ Three
And three times three repeat   ⎭ times.
  Jehovah's praise.

DEDICATION.

[ARLINGTON. C. M.]   DR. ARNE.

1ST TENOR.

1. Whilst science yields a thousand lights T'ir - ra - di - ate the mind,

2D TENOR.

1ST BASS.

2. The pompous dome, the gorgeous hall, The temple's cloud-capt tower,

2D BASS.

Let us that no - blest art pur-sue, Which dig - ni - fies man - kind.

The Ma-son's glo - ry shall proclaim, Till time's re - mot - est hour.

3 Ideal fabrics to uprear,
  Some men think all our art;
But little think what plans we draw,
  To form an upright heart.

4 Our plumb we poise, and clear each clog
  That hangs about the string; |
And each unruly passion's flight
  Within due compass bring.

5 The Good Samaritan we prove
  To all and everywhere;
Upon the level here we meet,
  And part upon the square.

6 Upon this rock we'll stand when worlds
  T' oblivion all shall tend;
Our brethren as ourselves we love;
  To all mankind a friend.

DEDICATION.

[MENDON. L. M.]

1st TENOR.

1. Master Supreme! ac - cept our praise; Still bless this con - se - cra - ted band;

2D TENOR.

2. May Faith, Hope, Chari - ty, di - vine, Here hold their un - di - vi - ded reign;
3. May Wisdom here dis - ci - ples find, Beau-ty un - fold her thousand charms,

1st BASS.

4. May Pi - ty dwell with - in each breast, Re - lief at - tend the suffering poor;

2D BASS.

Pa - rent of Light! il - lume our ways, And guide us' by thy sovereign hand.

Friendship and Har - mo - ny com-bine To soothe our care and ban - ish pain.
Sci - ence in - vig - or - ate the mind, Ex-pand the soul that vir - tue warms.

Thousands by this, our Lodge, be blest, Till worth, distrest, shall want no more.

45   INSTALLATION OR DEDICATION. L. M.

1 Ye happy few, who here extend
In perfect lines, from east to west,
With fervent zeal the Lodge defend,
And lock its secrets in each breast.

2 Since ye are met upon the square,
Bid love and friendship jointly reign;
Be peace and harmony your care,
Nor break the adamantine chain.

3 Behold the planets, how they move,
Yet keep due order as they run;
Then imitate the stars above,
And shine resplendent as the sun.

4 Then let us celebrate the praise
Of all who have enriched the art;
Let gratitude our voices raise,
And each true brother bear a part.

[AMERICA. 6s & 4s.]

1st Tenor.

1. Hail! brother Masons, hail! Let friendship long prevail, And bind us fast; May harmo-

2d Tenor.

2. We on the level meet, And every brother greet, Skilled in our art; And when our

1st Bass

3. May Wisdom be our care, And Virtue form the square By which we live; That we at

2d Bass

ny and peace Our happiness increase, And friendship never cease, While life doth last.

labor's past, Each brother's hand we'll grasp, Then on the square at last, Friendly we'll part.

last may join The Heavenly Lodge sublime, Where we shall perfect shine With God above.

47 [NATIONAL HYMN. 6s & 4s.]

1. My country, 'tis of thee.
Sweet land of liberty,
　Of thee I sing;
Land where my fathers died;
Land of the pilgrim's pride;
From every mountain side
　Let freedom ring.

2 My native country, thee,
Land of the noble free,
　Thy name I love;
I love thy rocks and rills,
Thy woods and templed hills;
My heart with rapture thrills
　Like that above.

3 Let music swell the breeze,
And ring from all the trees
　Sweet freedom's song;
Let mortal tongues awake;
Let all that breathe partake;
Let rocks their silence break—
　The sound prolong.

4 Our fathers' God, to thee
Author of Liberty,
　To thee we sing:
Long may our land be bright
With freedom's holy light;
Protect us by thy might,
　Great God, our King.

INSTALLATION HYMN.

[NUREMBURG. 7s.]

1ST TENOR.

1. Un - to thee, Great God, be - long   Mys - tic rites, and sa - cred song;

2D TENOR.

2. Glo-rious Arch - i - tect, a - bove, Source of Light, and source of Love!

1ST BASS.

3. Still to us, O God! dis-pense Thy di - vine be - nev - o - lence;

2D BASS.

Low - ly bend - ing at thy shrine, Hail, thou Ma - jes - ty di - vine!

Here thy light and love pre - vail, Hail! Al - mighty Mas - ter, hail!

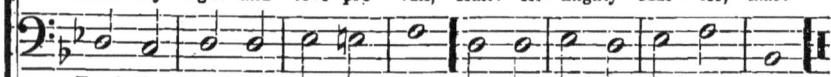

Teach the ten - der tear to flow, Melt - ing at a brother's woe.

---

4 Heavenly Father, grant that we,
Blest with boundless charity,
To th' admiring world may prove,
Happy they who dwell in love.

5 Join, on Earth ; and as you roll,
East to West, from pole to pole,
Lift to Him your grateful lays,
Join the universal praise.

49 OPENING OR CLOSING. 7s.

1 Softly now the light of day
Fades upon our sight away ;
Free from care, from labor free,
Lord, we would commune with thee.

2 Soon for us the light of day
Shall forever pass away ;
Then, from care and sorrow free,
Take us, Lord, to dwell with thee.

INSTALLATION.

[DEDHAM. C. M.]

1st Tenor.

1. To him who rules be hom - age paid, Where hearts with voice u - nite;

2d Tenor.

2. Come, brothers, bound by kind - ly ties, Your notes har - mo - nious bring,

1st Bass.

2d Bass.

To him we bring fra - ter - nal aid Who guides in so - lemn rite.

While acts of generous sa - cri - fice, In thoughts of love we sing.

3 As days and years roll silent by,
As times sad changes rise,
No doubt shall dim the trusting eye,
Where rule the good and wise.

4 To him who rules be homage paid,
Where hearts with voice unite;
Till life shall cease, and time shall fade,
We'll bring our solemn plight.

50 OPENING OR CLOSING. C. M.

1 Sweet is the memory of the night
When first we saw the light;
Dear to our souls shall ever be
The rite of Masonry.

2 Let Masons then, with watchful eye,
Regard true Charity;
Let Union, Love and Friendship meet
And show that wisdom's sweet.

INSTALLATION. CLOSING.

[WILL YOU BE THERE? C. P. M.]   J. W. DADMUN.

1ST TENOR.

1. When heaven's Great Arch - i - tect Di - vine Raised world on world in kind de-

2D TENOR.

2. While wandering on our clouded way, Com - pan - ion shed its kind - ly

1ST BASS.

3. With skill to work, and wise to guide, No pain shall come, no thought di-

2D BASS.

sign, Then form on earth was laid; Fra - ter - nal thoughts conferred on

ray, A guide to lead the blind; Con - duct - ed by a ho - ly

vide, Where hearts with heart a - gree; Then let us to our al - tar

man, By love inspired the so - cial plan, And so - cial hearts o - beyed.

light, With generous love and mys - tic rite, The pur - est joys we find.

bring The dear-est offering, while we sing, U - ni - ted, true and free.

---

52 INSTALLATION. C. P. M.

1 When darkness veiled the hopes of man,
Then light with radiant beams began
　To cheer his clouded way;
In graceful form, to soothe his woes,
The Beauty to his vision rose,
　In bright and gentle ray.

2 Immortal Order stood confessed,
From furthest East to distant West,
　In columns just and true;
The faithful Plumb and Level there,
Uniting with the mystic Square,
　The Temple brought to view.

3 Descending then from heaven, Most High,
Came Charity with tearful eye
　To dwell with feeble man;
Hope whispered peace in brighter skies,
On which a trusting Faith relies,
　And earth's best joys began.

4 Abroad was seen the boon of Heaven,
Fraternal Love was kindly given,
　And touched each kindred heart;

The Sons of Light with transport then,
In kindness to their fellow men,
　Unveiled the Mystic Art.

5 Let grateful peans loudly raise
O'er earth's domains, to azure skies,
　As time shall onward move;
A brother's joy and we shall be
Undying bonds to mark the Free,
　To wake a brother's Love.

56 INSTALLATION. C. P. M.

1 Hail, Mystic Light! whose holy flame
Can cheer the weak, the fierce can tame,
　And raise the trembling soul!
Hail, sacred source of human skill!
Hail, great director of the will!
　Star of the mental pole.

2 Hail! Masonry! thou first, thou last,
Of all the scope my mind embraced;
　Thou, teacher, friend, and guide;
Around thine altar now we stand,
In union strong, a loving band;
　Thus will we e'er abide.

INSTALLATION.

[SCOTS, WHA HAE WI'? 7s & 6s.]

1ST TENOR.

1. Mark where friends u - ni - ted stand, True of heart and free of hand!

2D TENOR.

2. While in kind - ness gathered here, Voic - es joined, and hearts sin - cere,

3. Who, that joys of friendship know, Who, that feels for oth - ers' woe,

1ST BASS.

4. Gath - er, then, with hearts up-right, Where the East gives forth its light;

2D BASS.

Broth - ers own his just com-mand, Who rules in so - cial hour:

Dis-cord's notes be nev - er near, Bring-ing thoughts un - kind:

Who, when tears of sor - row flow, Cold - ly turn a - way?

Give we now our so - lemn plight, In fra - ter - nal love:

Hark! he calls! o - be - dient now, Still and si - lent - ly we bow,

Con-stant to our so - cial tie, Hon - or beams from ev - ery eye;
At the words, in whis-pers told, That to broth - ers truth un - fold,

Soon, our earth - ly la - bors o'er, Bliss im - mor - tal yet in store,

Love impressed on ev - ery brow; We own his right - ful power.

Who, that shall his trust de - ny, Manhood's grace shall find?
Who would grate - ful thanks withhold, Who would friends be - tray!

Each shall find a hap - pier shore, Blessed with light a - bove.

[INSTALLATION. 11s.]

1ST TENOR.

INSTALLATION OF MASTER.

Sup - port to the Mas - ter, who rules by the Square,

2D TENOR.

INSTALLATION OF SENIOR WARDEN.

Sup - port to the War - den in - stalled in the West,

1ST BASS.

INSTALLATION OF JUNIOR WARDEN.

Sup - port to the War - den, by Plumb still up - right,

2D BASS.

Let sons of the Light to the East now re - pair;

Who works by the Lev - el, when sor - rows may rest;

Whose sun, in the South, nev - er hides its fair light;

With hearts for his aid, now u - ni - ted and free,

With hearts for his aid, now u - ni - ted and free,

With hearts for his aid, now u - ni - ted and free,

O - be - dient wo la - bor and kind - ly a - gree.

O - be - dient we la - bor and kind - ly a - gree.

O - be - dient wo la - bor and kind - ly a - gree.

CONSECRATION.

[SHIRLAND. S. M.]

1ST TENOR.

1. Great source of light and love, To Thee our songs we raise!

2D TENOR.

1ST BASS.

2. Shine on this fes - tive day, Suc - ceed its hoped de - sign,

2D BASS.

O, in thy tem - ple, Lord, a - bove, Hear and ac-cept our praise.

And may our Char - i - ty dis - play A love re - sem-bling thine.

3 May this fraternal band,
{ Now Consecrated—blest,
In Union all distinguished stand,
In Purity be drest.

4 May all the sons of peace
Their every grace improve,
Till discord through the nations cease.
And all the world be love

56 OPENING HYMN. S. M.

1 Kind Father ! hear our prayer,—
We bow before thy throne ;
O may we find acceptance there,
And peace before unknown.

2 Within these walls may Peace
And Harmony be found ;
May Faith and Charity increase,
And Hope and Love abound

GRAND LODGE.

[JOSEPH. C. M.]

From Mehul.

1st Tenor.

Fine.

1. As - sembled for sweet coun-cil now, Our craft in love to guide,
From dis - tant hills and sun - ny plains, Where faithful hearts re - side,
D.C. There's noth-ing like the tie we own To bind in un - ion true!

2d Tenor.

2. No dis-tance dims its lus - tre here, No climes its beau-ty fade;
For time, that wastes, all oth - er things, Its guardian hope is made;
D.C. There's noth-ing like the tie we own To bind in un - ion true!

1st Bass.

3. May all to our fair al - tar bring The dear - est offer-ing now:
The pledge that marks the good and true, The kind, fra - ter - nal vow:
D.C. There's noth-ing like the tie we own To bind in un - ion true!

2d Bass.

D.C.

With thoughts most kind and truth sin - cere, We here our pledge re - new:

And Truth, that forms its fair - est gem, Shall be our pass-word through:

In that Grand Lodge be - yond this world We'll pledge our vow a - new:

58   CLOSING. C. M.

1 Hail Masonry! thou sacred art
    Of origin divine!
Kind partner of each social heart,
    And favorite of the Nine!
By thee we're taught our acts to square,
    To measure life's short span;
And each infirmity to bear
    That's incident to man.

2 Tho' envy's tongue would blast thy fame,
    And simple ignorance sneer,
Yet still thy ancient, honored name,
    To each true brother's dear;
Then strike the blow, to charge prepare,
    In this we all agree,
May freedom be each Mason's care,
    And every Mason free.

PART II. CHAPTER.

MARK MASTER.

[STERLING. L. M.]

1st Tenor.

1. Ac-cept, GREAT BUILDER of the skies, Our heart-felt acts of sac - ri - fice!

2d Tenor.

2. Let ho - ly love our work still be, In - spir - ing hopes that rest on THEE!

1st Bass.

3. While Craftsmen true their work prepare, With thoughts unstained, and holy care,

2d Bass.

Each Brother found a liv - ing stone, While bending low be - fore Thy throne.

Thus, when we see a Brother's woe, Our hearts shall feel the love we owe.

May each be fit - ly formed, and placed Where LOVE DIVINE his hopes had traced.

60 MARK MASTERS' LODGE.

[OPENING.]

(Music on page 22. 6s & 4s.)

1 MARK MASTERS, gather near;
Hail our Grand Overseer,
  With heart and voice ;
Each in his station known
As some fair corner-stone,
Before our MASTER's throne,
  Let all rejoice !
CHO. Each in his station, &c.

2 May the GRAND ARCHITECT
Keep us, as sons elect,
  While time shall stand ;
To heaven our prayers shall rise,
In grateful sacrifice,
All hearts to solemnize
  In friendship's band.
CHO. To heaven, &c.

61 PAST MASTERS' LODGE.

[OPENING.]

(Music on page 38. 6s & 4s.)

1 Come, and with generous will,
Past Masters, bring your skill,
  Our work to prove ;
Calm each invading storm,
Each erring thought reform,
With Truth each bosom warm,
  Inspired by love.
CHO. Calm each, &c.

2 Firm as our columns stand,
Be each approved command,
  Where Brothers dwell ;
Let notes of kindness roll
Over each trusting soul;
Far as from pole to pole,
  Let anthems swell !
CHO. Let notes, &c.

62 PAST MASTER CANDIDATE.

[STERLING. L. M.]

1 Come, gather round, with hearts sincere,
While prayers devout are offered here;
In peace to rule, in truth to guide,
Let kindness o'er our acts preside.

2 To HIM, our HEAVENLY MASTER, now
With thoughts subdued, we humbly bow ;
So to our chosen Master here
Let true obedience still appear.

3 When, all our earthly labors o'er,
Our earthly Masters rule no more,
May each in holier climes find rest,
Where cares ne'er come, nor foes molest.

63 MOST EXCELLENT MASTERS' LODGE.

[OPENING].

(Music on page 22. 6s & 4s.)

1 See, from the Orient rise
Bright beams to bless our eyes,
  All hearts to cheer !
Let all, with one consent,
Impelled by true intent,
Become most Excellent,
  In love sincere.
CHO. Let all, &c.

2 Where rise our Temple-spires,
Bring hearts with pure desires—
  Offerings most true !
Whate'er in time shall be,
Let all the good and free,
Faithful to HEAVEN's decree,
  Their vows renew.
CHO. Whate'er in time, &c.

MARK MASTER'S SONG.

[AMERICA. 6s & 4s.]

1st Tenor.

1. Mark Masters all appear, Before the Chief O'erseer, In concert move; Let him your

2d Tenor.

2. You, who have pass'd the Square, For your rewards prepare, Join heart and hand; Each with his

1st Bass.

3. Hiram, the widow's son, Sent un-to Sol-o-mon Our great key-stone; On it ap-

2d Bass.

work inspect, For the Chief Architect; If there be no de-fect, He will approve.

mark in view, March with the just and true; Wages to you are due, At your command.

pears the name That raises high the fame Of all to whom the same Is tru-ly known.

4 Now to the Westward move,
Where, full of strength and love,
   Hiram doth stand;
But if impostors are
Mix'd with the worthy there,
Caution them to beware
   Of the right hand.

5 Now to the praise of those
Who triumphed o'er the foes
   Of Mason's arts;
To the praiseworthy three,
Who founded this Degree:
May all their virtues be
   Deep in our hearts.

MARK MASTER.

[OLD HUNDRED. L. M.]

An - oth - er six days' work is done; An - oth - er Sab - bath is be - gun;

An - oth - er six days' work is done; An - oth - er Sab - bath is be - gun;

Re - turn, my soul, en - joy thy rest; Im - prove the day thy God hath bless'd.

Re - turn, my soul, en - joy thy rest: Im - prove the day thy God hath bless'd.

MARK MASTER. (CLOSING.)

1 Accept, Great Builder of the skies,
Our heartfelt acts of sacrifice!
Each brother found a living stone,
While bending low before thy throne.

2 While craftsmen true their work prepare,
With thoughts unstained, and holy care,
May each be fitly formed and placed
Where Love Divine his hopes had traced

MOST EXCELLENT MASTER'S SONG.

[PORTUGUESE HYMN. 11s.]

1st Tenor.

1. All hail to the morning That bids us re - joice; The Tem-ple's com - plet-ed, Ex-

2d Tenor.

1st Bass.

2. To th' Power Almighty, Who ever has guid - ed The tribes of old Israel, ex-

2d Bass.

alt high each voice: The cap-stone is finish'd, Our la - bor is o'er; The sound of the

alting their fame; To Him who hath govern'd our hearts undivided, Let's send forth our

gavel, The sound of the gavel, The sound of the gavel Shall hail us no more.

voices, Let's send forth our voices, Let's send forth our voices To praise his great Name.

Companions assemble
On this joyful day;
(The occasion is glorious,)
The key-stone to lay :
Fulfill'd is the promise,
By the ANCIENT OF DAYS,
To bring forth the cap-stone
With shouting and praise.

[CEREMONIES.]

There's no more occasion
For level or plumb-line,
For trowel or gavel,
For compass or square ;
Our works are completed,
The ark safely seated,
And we shall be greeted
As workmen most rare.

Now those that are worthy,
Our toils who have shar'd,
And prov'd themselves faithful,
Shall meet their reward
Their virtue and knowledge,
Industry and skill,
Have our approbation,
Have gain'd our good will.

We accept and receive them,
Most Excellent Masters,
Invested with honors,
And power to preside ;
Among worthy Craftsmen,
Wherever assembled,
The knowledge of Masons
To spread far and wide.

ALMIGHTY JEHOVAH!
Descend now and fill
This lodge with thy glory,
Our hearts with good will !
Preside at our meetings,
Assist us to find
True pleasure in teaching
Good will to mankind.

Thy Wisdom inspired
The great Institution,
Thy strength shall support it,
Till nature expire ;
And when the creation
Shall fall into ruin,
Its Beauty shall rise,
. Through the midst of the fire !

ROYAL ARCH.

[WELTON. L. M.]

1st Tenor.

1. While wandering on life's darksome way, Pro-tect us HEAVENLY KING, we pray!

2d Tenor.

2. When threatening dangers press around, When Hope gives back no cheer-ing sound,

1st Bass.

3. Thus when our rug-ged path we tread, By Thy kind spir-it gent-ly led,

2d Bass.

In mer-cy, then, O guide our feet, In midnight hour or noon-day heat!

Be THOU, our FATHER, kind-ly near, And free our hearts from ev-ery fear.

In dan-gers of a world like this, Our faith shall dwell on fu-ture bliss.

69 ROYAL ARCH. [CLOSING. GREENVILLE. 8s & 7s.]

1 Lowly now we bend before THEE,
 HOLY GUIDE in life's dark way!
GREAT HIGH PRIEST! may each adore THEE,
 Led by Truth's unerring ray!
CHO. Lowly now we bend before THEE,
 HOLY GUIDE in life's dark way!

2 Grateful thanks in hearts are swelling,
 While protection still we pray:
Still be heard the thanks we're telling,
 As the scenes of time decay.
CHO. Lowly now we bend before THEE,
 HOLY GUIDE in life's dark way!

[GOLDEN HILL. S. M.]

1st Tenor.

1. Blest are the thoughts that bind In kind, fra - ter - nal ties,

2d Tenor.

2. Though dan - gers mark our way, And dark - ness dim our course,

1st Bass.

3. Be - fore our GREAT HIGH PRIEST Our offerings now we bear;

2d Bass.

Where al - tars raised to love shall find The hearts best sac - ri - fice!

Com - pan - ions see, in Truth's fair ray, Their pleasure's dear - est source.

And still, when hopes of time have ceased, We'll pay our hom - age there.

---

71   RED CROSS. L. M.   (Music on page 42.)

(Music on page 42.)

1 Ah! when shall we three meet like them,
Who last were at Jerusalem?
For one lies low, alas! he's not,
The green Accacia marks the spot.

2 Though poor he was, with kings he trod';
Though great, he humbly knelt to God :
Ah! when shall hope restore again.
The broken link of friendship's chain.

3 Behold! where mourning beauty bent
In silence o'er his monument,
And wildly spread, in sorrow there,
The ringlets of her flowing hair.

4 From whence we come, or whither go,
Ask me no more, or seek to know,
Till three shall meet, who formed like them,
The Grand Lodge of Jerusalem.

CONSTITUTING A CHAPTER.

[BETHLEHEM. 8s & 7s.] SPANISH AIR.

1ST TENOR.

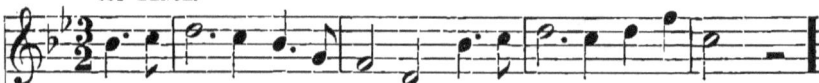

1. Closely bound in ties fra-ter-nal, On our rug-ged way we go;

2D TENOR.

1ST BASS.

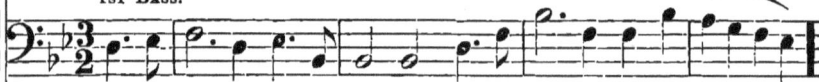

2. Ev-er thus, to friends u-ni-ted, Be our ties each coming year;

2D BASS.

Scattered there like blossoms ver-nal, Hopes their gen-tle boon be-stow.

D. S. Grateful, too, the joys pro-mot-ed, Dear-er seen in pass-ing years.

Like the Ho-ly Flame that light-ed Love to God in hearts sin-cere.

D. S. Then, on Heaven our hope re-pos-ing, Sorrows shall no more in-vade.

Peaceful are the hours de - vot - ed Where the glori - ous Arch ap - pears!

When at last in time's sad clos - ing, Temples cease and Arches fade,

---

73 OPENING. 8s & 7s.

1 When the light of day is waning,
To this place we oft repair;
Here we all unite in singing,
Here devoutly join in prayer :
While in harmony our voices
Are ascending to our God,
Every grateful heart rejoices
Thus to spread his praise abroad.

2 In the duties now before us,
Let us faithfully engage ;
May the light of Truth shine o'er us,
Brightly from the sacred page:
Father! thus in pure devotion,
Every thought inspired by love,
Gratitude in each emotion,
Would we lift our souls above.

74 ROYAL ARCH CHAPTER. 6s & 4s.

(Music on page 22.)

1 Where burns the Sacred Fire.
Each heart, with pure desire,
Bring thoughts of love !
Who, with affections cold,
Would highest praise withhold,
When Hope's best joys unfold
The bliss above ?

2 While to our HEAVENLY KING
Hearts filled with love we bring,
Come, join in praise !

'Neath heaven's broad arch of blue,
Where dwell the free and true,
There our best vows anew
In anthems raise!

75 PLACING KEY-STONE. 6s & 4s,

(Music on page 22.)

1 Placed now in form most true
Our finished work we view,
With hearts sincere :
Long be the Key-Stone found
Grateful to all around,
As notes of joy resound,
In accents clear.

2 While years roll silent by,
Pointing our Hope on high
There let it stand :
There may the good and great,
With fondest joys elate,
Faith's promised bliss await,
At HEAVEN's command.

3 When, our last labor o'er,
Scenes of this life no more
Charm our frail sight,
Then in God's holy care
May each protection share,
Bliss found unending there
In Perfect Light.

PART III. ENCAMPMENT.

RED CROSS COUNCIL.

[SICILIAN HYMN. 8s & 7s.]

1ST TENOR.

1. Bring your offer - ing to our Tem-ple! Let the in - cense reach the skies!

2D TENOR.

2. Bring af - fec - tion kind-ly tempered, Hearts to join a kindred heart,

1ST BASS.

3. Bring de - vo - tion, free, in - spir - ing, High resolves and ho - ly thought;

2D BASS.

Ju - dah's line, no more a stranger, Sees its ho - ly al - tars rise.

Heavenly Truth their worthiest ob - ject, Christian Faith their worthiest part.

Seek to gain the worthy conquest By a Saviour's sufferings bought.

4 Bring in hearts of generous purpose,
Charity's endearing form ;
Love enlarged, mankind embracing,
Ever faithful, active, warm.

5 Bring, O, bring a Brother's welfare
On the purest breath of prayer ! —
Thus when passed o'er life's frail confines,
Man shall find his heaven there.

[REST. L. M.]

1st Tenor.

1. Come, hail the Prince of Ju-dah's line, Inspired by Truth and Love di - vine!

2d Tenor.

1st Bass.

2. No more shall tears un - kind - ly flow, No more complaints shall true hearts know;

2d Bass.

When dark op - pres-sion held its sway, His courage gave a bright-er day.

Our beauteous Tem-ple rising near, Where thanks shall live in hearts sin - cere.

3 With thoughts most kind, our trust on high,
Companions for a brighter sky!
The Cross our emblem, HEAVEN our guide,
No fear shall come, no foes divide.

4 Be every act and purpose seen
Like Truth, that holds immortal green,
Where fairest blossoms gathered here
In brighter hues shall yet appear!

78 RED CROSS COUNCIL. L. M.

1 From hearts sincere, from lips most true,
We bring united thanks anew;
Be all our hopes reposed on THEE,
While time shall last, or Truth shall be.

2 While humbly now our homage owned
To HIM, our SOVEREIGN, high enthroned,
O, be our footsteps guided still
Where truth shall dearest hopes fulfill !

RED CROSS COUNCIL.

[GANGES. C. P. M.]

1ST TENOR.

1. Our songs of praise we grateful bring   To Ju - dah's line and Per-sia's king,

2D TENOR.

1ST BASS.

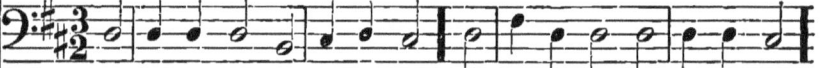

2. No more complaints, no sorrowing tears,   No ser - vile chains, nor cap - tive fears,

2D BASS.

That gave the builders   aid :   When arch and column   pros - trate fell,

Their joy-less hours shall find :   U - ni - ted songs from hearts se - rene,

Hope bade the song of tri-umph swell, And Is-rael's hosts o-beyed.

When-e'er in Coun-cil friends con-vene, In closer ties shall bind.

80 ENCAMPMENT. C. P. M.

1 Come, soldier of the cross, draw nigh,
With manly arm and pitying eye,
  To guard the pilgrim band ;
Though countless foes shall gather round,
Still be the valiant Templar found
  Where duty shall command.

2 To orphan's cry and woman's woe,
We'll gently bear the boon we owe,
  When true to Knighthood's claim ;
Though dangers mark our onward way,
No foe we'll fear, nor friends betray,
  But seek the good man's name.

81 ANNIVERSARY. C. P. M.

1 See in the East effulgent shine,
Bright wisdom with his rays divine,
  Hark ! hark, the solemn sound ;
While thus we live in mutual love,
We taste what angels do above,—
  Here happiness is found.

2 The fruit of Eden's tree we taste,
Its balmy joys are our repast,
  Here freedom cheers the heart ;
The indigent, oppressed with grief,
Gains from his brother's hand relief,
  Each to his want impart.

3 The great and good with us combine
To trace our mysteries divine,
  And find the pleasing light ;
With pleasure we pursue the plan,
While friendship rivets man to man,
  How pleasing is the sight.

4 Till Heaven sends its summons forth,
From east to west, from south to north,
  Her chosen sons to call ;
While time runs its continual round,
Shall fame with golden trumpet sound,
  Masons shall never fall.

82 CLOSING. C. P. M.

1 We help the poor in time of need,
The naked clothe, the hungry feed,
  'T is our foundation stone :
We build upon the noblest plan,
For friendship rivets man to man,
  And makes us all as one

2 Still louder, Fame ! thy trumpet blow ;
Let all the distant regions know
  Free-Masonry is this :
Almighty Wisdom gave it birth,
And Heaven has fixed it here on earth,
  A type of future bliss !

ENCAMPMENT.

[PETERBORO'. C. M.]

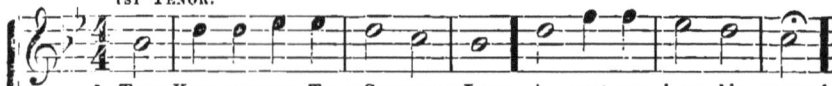

1ST TENOR.

1. Thou King of kings, Thou Sovereign Lord, Ac - cept our hum - ble prayer!

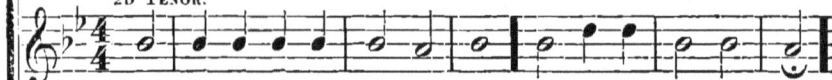

2D TENOR.

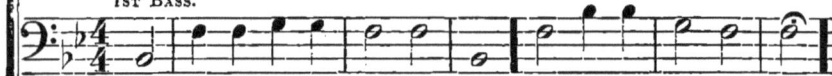

1ST BASS.

2. A ris - en Savior here we own, Who passed the si - lent grave;

2D BASS.

While travelling on life's dangerous road, O, still pro - tect us there!

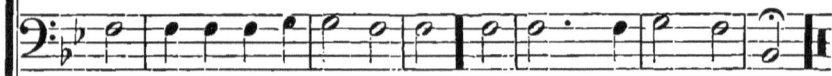

His love im - mor - tal kind - ly shown, Who came a world to save.

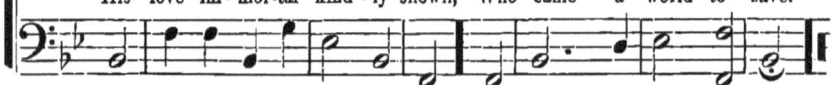

3 When weary Pilgrims, travelling far
  Shall seek thy holy light,
Be Thou, O God, that guiding star,
  Ne'er dimmed by shades of night,

4 Be Truth's kind hand forever nigh
  Each Pilgrim faint to stay,
No darkness cloud his trusting eye,
  Nor sorrow mark his way!

80 ENCAMPMENT. C. M.

1 How glorious is the gift of Faith,
  That cheers the darksome tomb,
And through the damp and gloomy grave
  Can shed a rich perfume!

2 Triumphant Faith! it lifts the soul
  Above desponding fear;
Exults in hope of heaven, her home,
  And longs to enter there!

ENCAMPMENT.

[DORT.   6s & 4s.]

1ST TENOR.

2D TENOR.

1. The laws of Christian light, These are our weapons bright, Our mighty shield; Christ is our

1ST BASS.

2D BASS.

leader high, And the broad plains which lie Beneath the blessed sky Our battle-field.

2 On, then, in God's great name ;
Let each pure spirit's flame
Burn bright and clear :
Stand firmly in your lot,
Cry ye aloud, "doubt not"!
Be every fear forgot,
Christ leads us here.

3 So shall earth's distant lands,
In happy, holy bands,
One brotherhood,
Together rise and sing,
And joyful offerings bring,
And heaven's eternal King
Pronounce it good.

86   "LET THERE BE LIGHT."   6s & 4s.

1 Let there be light ! Said God;
And o'er the blooming sod
Broke forth the Morn !
Glad nature smiled in mirth,
While beauty filled the earth,
And flowers were born !

2 Let there be light within ;
Then darkness, woe, and sin,
Your night is riven :
Then in pale sorrow's eve,
The startling tear relieve ;
O speed it, Heaven

KNIGHTS TEMPLARS.

Words by H. G. BARROWS. [PLEYEL'S HYMN. 7s.]

1ST TENOR.

1. To thy shrine, de-part-ed Lord, Come we, trust-ing in thy word;

2D TENOR.

2. Strong in Faith, and Hope, and Love, Lift we now our thoughts a-bove;

1ST BASS.

3. Let thy light up-on us shine; Fill our hearts with love di-vine;

2D BASS.

In thy serv-ice rich-ly blest, Here, we pray thee, let us rest.

To thy serv-ice pure and free, Let us con-se-cra-ted be.

On thy arm we trust our all, Keep us, that we nev-er fall.

---

88 KNIGHTS TEMPLARS.

1 Angels! roll the rock away!
Death! yield up thy mighty prey!
See! he rises from the tomb,
Rises with immortal bloom.

2 'T is the Saviour—seraphs, raise
Your triumphant shouts of praise;
Let the earth's remotest bound
Hear the joy-inspiring sound.

3 Praise him, all ye heavenly choirs,
Praise. and sweep your golden lyres,
Praise him in the noblest songs,
Praise him from ten thousand tongues.

89 KNIGHTS TEMPLARS.

1 Lord, before thy throne we bend,
Now to thee our eyes ascend:
Servants to our Master true,
Lo! we yield thee homage due.

2 Low before thee, Lord, we bow,
We are weak—but mighty thou:
Sore distressed, yet suppliant still,
Here we wait thy holy will.

3 Leave us not beneath the power
Of temptation's darkest hour;
Heavenly Father, yet be nigh.
Lord of life and victory.

Words by H. G. BARROWS. [GREENVILLE. 8s & 7s.]

1ST TENOR.

Melody in 2D TENOR. Fine.

1. Fare-well, pilgrim, Heaven protect thee, Guide thy footsteps on the way;
Trust in God, then, He'll de - fend thee, Bring thee to the light of day.

1ST BASS.

2D BASS. Fine.

D.C.

Tho' thy path be sad and drea - ry, Soon shall rise the light of day.

D.C.

2 Let the Saviour's bright example
  Cheer thy sorrow-burdened heart;
Trust in God, thy only refuge,
  He will peace and joy impart.
Be not weary in well-doing,
  God can cheer the saddest heart.

3 On, then, through thy TOUR OF PENANCE,
  Cast thy every fear away;
God shall guide thee, who hath never
  Led one pilgrim's feet astray.
Trust in Him and He shall guide thee,
  Safely guide thee on thy way.

THE MAUSOLEUM.

[WATCHMAN. S. M.]

1. How dark the road we go To our last rest-ing-place!

2. Our FATHER, hear our cry! To THEE, to THEE we pray;

There all we hold so dear be-low Is lost in death's embrace.

Our trust-ing hearts on THEE re-ly When life's best hopes de-cay!

3 No proudly nodding plume,
   No banner waving high,
Can stay the sadness of the tomb,
   Or hush a rising sigh.

4 But Hope, with holy aid,
   'Mid sadness gathering there,
Pours gentle light on grief's deep shade,
   And finds relief in prayer.

5 See where a SAVIOR's love
   That sacred Hope decreed!
That man should live in bliss above,
   Though dying hear him plead!

6 Be that immortal light
   Still radiant o'er the tomb!
The soul, upborne to mansions bright
   Shall find undying bloom!

KNIGHTS OF MALTA.

[RETREAT. L. M.]

1ST TENOR.

1. What Christian Knight, though dangers press, Unmanly fears would e'er confess!

2D TENOR.

1ST BASS.

2. His trust reposed on HEAVEN a-lone, No foes a-larm, no fears are known.

2D BASS.

'Mid gathering storms, when tempests roll, No ter-rors shake his trusting soul.

He sees in Faith that beaming star, That shone on Bethlehem's plains a-far.

3 Still faithful and believing found,
Where clouds and darkness gather round,
The Christian soldier onward moves,
Where duty leads, when HEAVEN approves.

4 In darkest hour, though death appear,
Without a sigh, without a tear,
Confiding still in HEAVEN's design,
He calmly owns the HAND DIVINE.

KNIGHTS OF MALTA. L. M.

1 To HIM, the GREAT JEHOVAH, now,
With holy awe we humbly bow;
Around the Cross, with hearts sincere,
We bring devotion's offering here.

2 What dearer offering shall we bring
To THEE, O God! our HEAVENLY KING!
When death shall come, our duty passed,
Then take us to thyself again.

KNIGHTS TEMPLARS. INSTALLATION.

Words by H. G. BARROWS. [WOODSTOCK. C. M.]

1. God of our fa-thers, hear the song Which now to thee we raise;

2. "IM-PAR-TIAL JUS-TICE," may it fill And ac-tu-ate each heart,

An evening of-fer-ing we bring, A song of grate-ful praise.

Aud lead us to de-fend, and take A wor-thy broth-er's part.

3 May FORTITUDE UNDAUNTED prove,
In journeying through life,
A power to make us ever bold,
'Midst every worldly strife.

4 May MERCY, brightest of the train,
Each knightly heart inspire,

And on the altar of each heart
Light love's celestial fire.

5 Throughout our pilgrimage, or us,
May thy choice blessings rest,
Until we enter thy abode,
Th' asylum of the blest.

FAITH, HOPE AND CHARITY. 57

Words by H. G. BARROWS. [MARTYRDOM. C. M.] SCOTCH.

1ST TENOR.

2D TENOR.

1. Oh bless-ed three, those gifts of heaven, With-in our hearts re-main;

1ST BASS.

2D BASS.

Let char - i - ty e'er reign su - preme, Di - vin - est of the train.

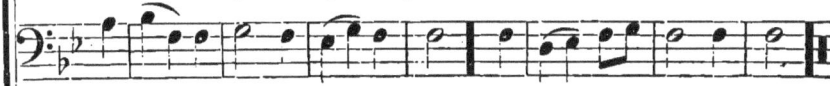

2 In SIGHT our faith may soon be lost,
   Hope in FRUITION ends!
But charity throughout this world,
   And to the next extends.

3 There it shall reign divinely pure,
   Amid the blest above,—
This theme pervades the songs of heaven,
   Where all the air is LOVE.

96 OPENING OR CLOSING. C M.

1 Sweet is the memory of the night
   When first we saw the light;
Dear to our souls shall ever be
   The rite of Masonry.

2 Let Masons then, with watchful eye,
   Regard true Charity;
Let Union, Love and Friendship meet,
   And show that wisdom's sweet.

GRAND ENCAMPMENT.

[ORLANDO. H. M.]

1st Tenor.

1. Come, ga - ther, Knights, a - round, For coun - cil kind - ly met, By

2d Tenor.

2 In peace u - nit - ed here, Let none our tent in - vade, No

1st Bass.

3. Then join, each trus - ty Knight, In coun - cil hours most kind; Let

2d Bass.

ties of hon - or bound, We nev - er can for - get: With lan - ces fair, With

thought unkind ap - pear, No act our hope de - grade; With lan - ces fair, With

hearts true hearts in - vite In hon - or's ties to bind. With lan - ces fair, With

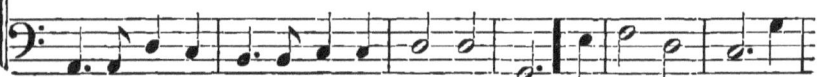

ban - ners bright, Shall truth de-clare, Shall truth de - clare The Templar Knight.

ban - ners bright, Shall truth de-clare, Shall Truth de - clare The Templar Knight.

ban - ners bright, Shall Truth de-clare, Shall Truth de - clare The Templar Knight.

97 OPENING ENCAMPMENT. ii. m.

1 Bring songs of joyous sound!
Bring hearts triumphant now!
Bring holy thoughts profound!
Devoutly let us bow!
Cho. To Him above
Let anthems rise,
Whose radiant Love
Fills earth and skies.

2 Awake, inspiring song!
Awake, celestial strain!
Let echo's voice prolong
Its note o'er hill and plain!
Cho. To Him, &c.

3 May hearts united find
Responsive blessings here!
No whispered word unkind
Create a rising tear.
Cho. To Him, &c.

4 Then come with joyous heart,
No sound of discord near;
Let forms of beauteous art
Yet rise triumphant here.
Cho. To Him, &c.

98 OPENING ENCAMPMENT. h. m.

(Music on page 22.)

1 Blest Art of Ancient fame!
Let echo's voice proclaim
The welcome word:

May this divine decree—
Man's dearest bond shall be
Indulgent Charity—
Still sound abroad.

2 When Chaos fled from earth,
Then Order first had birth
In forms of Light:
'Twas Wisdom's own behest,
That Strength should ever rest,
Where Beauty stood confessed,
In radiance bright.

3 Then God's most perfect plan,
In love to feeble man,
Was kindly given:
With Level, Plumb, and Square,
Form rose from rudeness there,
Proportions just and fair,
The boon of Heaven.

4 Should sorrow seek relief,
Then be another's grief
In mercy there ;
Kindness for human woe,
Soft pity's warmest glow,
Let each true Brother know,
Our constant care.

5 Come, join a Brother's joy;
In sweetest song employ
This festal day;
Let each fraternal tie
Its purest faith imply,
Our Hope still fixed on high,
In cloudless ray.

PART IV.

COUNCIL OF ROYAL AND SELECT MASTERS.

——

ROYAL MASTER.

[NASHVILLE. 7s.]   S. B. BALL.

1ST TENOR.
1. Joy! the sa - cred Law is found, Now the tem - ple stands com-plete,

2D TENOR.
2. Joy! the se - cret vault is found; Full the sun-beam falls with - in,

1ST BASS.
3. This shall be the cor - ner stone, Which the build-ers threw a - way,

2D BASS.

Glad - ly let us gath - er round, Where the Pon - tiff holds his seat.

Point - ing dark-ly un - der ground, To the trea - sure we would win.

But was found the on - ly one Fit - ted for the arch's stay.

[LANESBORO. C. M.]

1st Tenor.

2d Tenor.

1. Behold! how pleasant and how good, For brethren, such as we Of the ac - cept - ed

1st Bass.

2d Bass.

brotherhood, Of the ac - cept-ed broth - er - hood, To dwell in u - ni - ty.

2 'T is like the oil on Aaron's head,
  Which to his feet distils;
Like Hermon's dew, so richly shed
  On Zion's sacred hills.

3 For there the Lord of light and love
  A blessing sent with power;
Oh, may we all this blessing prove,
  E'en life forevermore.

4 On Friendship's altar, rising here,
  Our hands now plighted be,—
To live in Love with hearts sincere,
  In Peace and Unity.

101 SELECT MASTER.

1 How precious is the book divine,
  That unto us is given;
Bright as a lamp its doctrines shine,
  To guide our souls to heaven

2 It sweetly cheers our drooping hearts,
  In this dark vale of tears;
Life, light and joy it still imparts,
  And quells our rising fears.

3 This lamp, through all the tedious nigh,
  Of life, shall guide our way;
Till we behold the clearer light,
  Of an eternal day.

SUPER EXCELLENT MASTER.

[ST. MARTIN'S. C. M.]

1ST TENOR.

1. By Ba - bel's stream we sit and weep; Our tears for Zi - on flow;

2D TENOR.

1ST BASS.

[SQUARE.] 2. Our walls no more re - sound with praise; Our tem - ple foes de-stroy;

2D BASS.

Our harps on droop - ing wil-lows sleep; Our hearts are filled with woe.

Ju - de - a's courts no more up-raise Tri - umph - ant songs of joy.

[TRIANGLE.]

3 Here, mourning, toiling, captive bands,
   Our feasts and Sabbaths cease;
Our tribes dispersed through distant lands,
   And hopeless of release.

[CIRCLE.]

4 But should the ever-gracious Power
   To us propitious be;
Chaldeans shall our race restore,
   And kings proclaim us free.

SUPER EXCELLENT MASTER.

[EVENING HYMN. L. M.]

1ST TENOR.

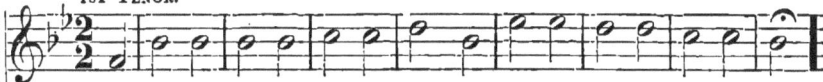

1. When we, our wearied limbs to rest, Sat down by proud Eu - phrates' stream,

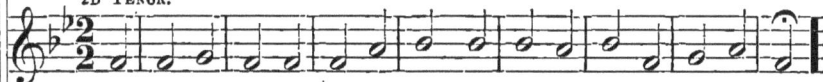

2D TENOR.

2. Our harps, that, when with joy we sung, Were wont their tune-ful parts to bear,

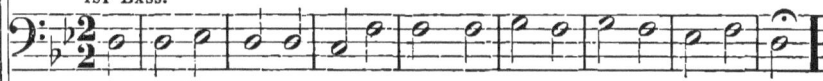

1ST BASS.

3. How shall we tune our voice to sing, Or touch our harps with skil-ful hands?

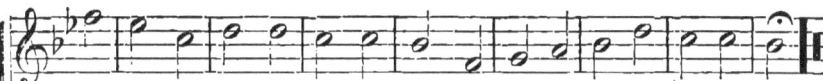

2D BASS.

We wept, with dole - ful thoughts oppressed, And Zi - on was our mourn-ful theme.

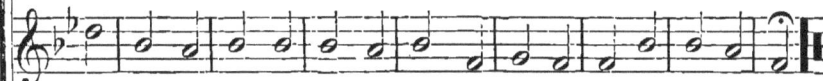

With si - lent strings, neg-lect - ed hung, On wil - low trees that withered there.

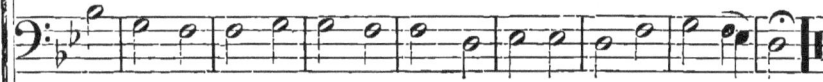

Shall hymns of joy, to God our King, Be sung by slaves in foreign lands?

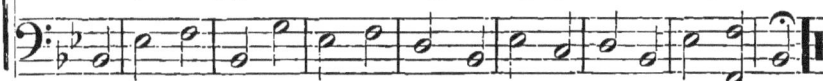

4 O Salem, our once happy seat!
   When I of thee forgetful prove,
Then let my trembling hand forget
   The tuneful strings with art to move.

5 If I to mention thee forbear,
   Eternal silence seize my tongue ;
Or if I sing one cheerful air,
   Till thy deliverance is my song.

INSTALLATION.

[ERIE. 7s.]

Fine.

1ST TENOR.

1. Fa - ther of the hu - man race, Wise, be - ne - fi - cent and kind,
Spread o'er na - ture's am - ple face, Flows thy goodness un - con - fined:
D.C. Still we trace thy wondrous love, Claim-ing large re - turns a - gain.

2D TENOR.

2. Lord, what offerings shall we bring At thine al - tars, when we bow?
Hearts, the pure un - sul - lied spring Whence the kind af - fec - tions flow;
D.C. Sym - pa - thy, at whose con - trol Sor-row leaves the wounded breast:

1ST BASS.

3. Will - ing hands to lead the blind, Heal the wounded, feed the poor;
Love, em - brac - ing all our kind; Char - i - ty with liberal store:
D.C. Thus th' ac-cept-ed offering bring,— Love to thee and all man-kind.

2D BASS.

D.C.

Mus - ing in the si - lent grove, Or the bus - y walks of men,

Soft compassion's feel - ing soul, By the melting eye expressed;

Teach us, O thou heavenly King. Thus to show our grate - ful mind,

PART V. MISCELLANEOUS.

CHANT. ENTERED APPRENTICE.

Ps. CXXXIII.

1ST TENOR.

1. Behold, how good and how .... pleasant it is

2D TENOR.

3. It is like the precious ointment up - - - - on the head,
5. That went down to the.................. skirts of his garments.

1ST BASS.

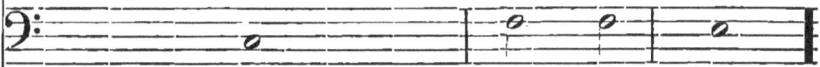

7. For there the Lord com - - - - mand - ed the blessing,

2D BASS.

2. For brethren to dwell to - - gether in u - ni - ty.

4. That ran down upon the........ beard, even Aa - ron's beard:
6. As the dew of Hermon, and as }
   the dew that descended up - - } on the moun-tains of Zion.

8. Even .... life for - ev - er - more. A - men.

CHANT. FELLOW CRAFT.

I. Cor. Chap. XIII.

1st Tenor.

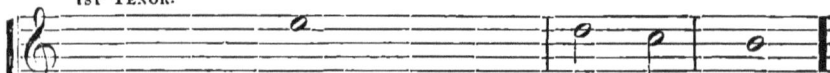

1. Though I speak with the tongues of .... men and of angels,
3. And though I have the gift of prophecy, and understand all mysteries, ... } and all knowledge:

2d Tenor.

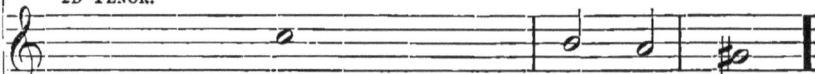

5. And though I bestow all my goods to.................. feed the poor,
7. Charity suffereth .... long, and is kind;
9. Doth not behave it - - - - - - self un - seemly,

1st Bass.

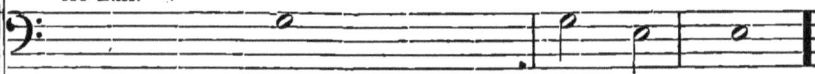

11. Rejoiceth not in in - - - - - - - i - qui - ty,
13. Beareth all things, be - - - - - - - lieveth all things,

2d Bass.

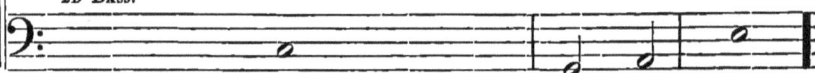

2. And have not charity, I am become as sounding .... } brass, or a tink - ling cymbal.
4. And though I have all faith, so that I could remove mountains, and have not ...... } chari - ty, I am nothing.

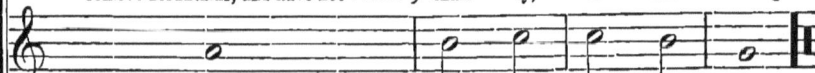

6. And though I give my body to be burned, and have not charity, it.............. } pro - fit - eth me nothing.
8. Charity envieth not; charity vaunteth not it - self, is not puffed up.
10. Seeketh not her own, is not easily pro - voked, doth not think evil;

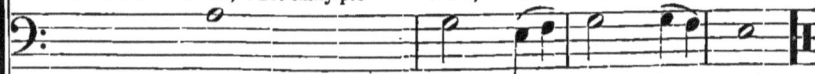

12. But re - - - - - - - joic - eth in the truth;
14. Hopeth all things, en - - - - - dur - - - eth all things.

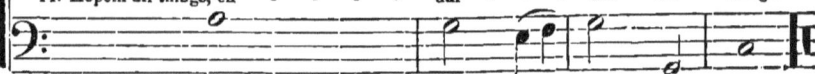

CHANT. FELLOW CRAFT.

Amos. VII. 7 & 8.

1st Tenor.

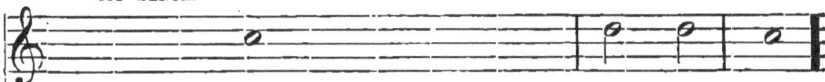

1. Thus he shewed me : and behold, the Lord stood upon a wall }
made by a .... } plumb - - line,

2d Tenor.

3. And the Lord said unto me, Amos, what .... seest...... thou ?

1st Bass.

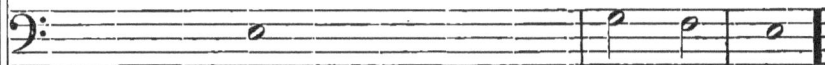

5. Then said the Lord, Behold, I will set a plumb-line in the }
midst of my people .... } Is - ra - el :

2d Bass.

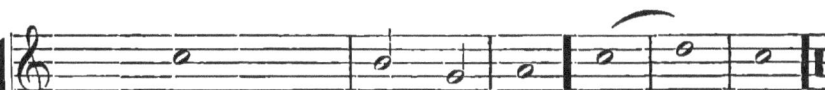

2. With a plumb-line .... in his hand.

4. And I said, A................ plumb - - line

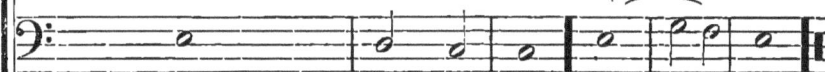

6. I will not again pass by them.... an - y more. A - - men.

CHANT. MASTER MASON.

ECCL. XII. 1 & 7.

1. Remember now thy Creator in the .... days of thy youth,
3. While the sun, or the light, or the moon, or the............ stars, be not darkened,
5. In the day when the keepers of the .... house shall tremble,

7. And those that look out of the............................ windows be darkened,
9. When the sound of the .... grinding is low,
11. Also when they shall be afraid of .... that which is high,

13. And the grass-hopper shall be a burden, and de - - - sire shall fail:
15. Or ever the silver cord be loosed, or the golden .... bowl be broken,
17. Then shall the dust return to the .... earth as it was:

2. While the evil days come not, nor the
   years draw nigh, when thou shalt say, I } have no pleas - ure in them.
4. Nor the clouds re - - - - - turn - - - - af - ter the rain.
6. And the strong men shall bow them-
   selves, and the grinders .... } cease, be - cause they are few,

8. And the .... doors shall be shut in the streets,
10. And he shall rise up at the voice of the
    bird, and all the daughters of music. } shall be brought.... low
12. And fears shall be in the way, and the al - mond tree shall flourish,

14. Because man goeth to his long
    home, and the mourners....... } go a - bout the streets:
16. Or the pitcher be broken at the
    fountain, or the.............. } wheel broken at the cistern.
18. And the spirit shall re - - turn unto God who gave it. A - men.

1. Glory be to .... God on high,
2. We praise thee, we bless thee, we .... wor - ship thee,
3. O Lord God, ... heaven - ly King,

4. O Lord, the only begotten Son, ... Je - sus Christ,
5. That takest away the .... sins of the world,
6. Thou that takest away the .... sins of the world,
7. Thou that takest away the .... sins of the world,

8. Thou that sittest at the right hand of .... God the Father,
9. For thou only .... art .... Holy,
10. Thou only, O Christ, with the .... Ho - ly Ghost,

and on earth .... peace, good will towards men.
we glorify thee, we give thanks to ...... thee, for thy great glory.
God the .... Fa - ther Al - - - mighty.

O Lord God, Lamb of God, ... Son .... of the Father.
have .... mer - cy up - on us.
have .... mer - cy up - on us.
re - - - - - - - ceive .... our .... prayer.

have .... mer - cy up - on us.
thou .... on - ly art the Lord.
art most high in the .... glory of God the Father.

CHANT. HE WAS DESPISED.

Isaiah. LIII. 3—6.

1st Tenor.

1. He was despised and.................... rejected of men,
3. And we hid as it were our .... fa - ces from him.
5. Surely he hath borne our griefs, and ...... carried our sorrows ;

2d Tenor.

7. But he was wounded for .... our trans - - gressions,
9. The chastisement of our .... peace was up - on him,

1st Bass.

11. All we like sheep have.................. gone a - - stray ;
13. And the Lord hath.................... laid on him

2d Bass.

2. A man of sorrows and ac - quaint - ed with...... grief.
4. He was despised, and..... we es - teemed him not.
6. Yet we did esteem him }
stricken, smitten of........ } God..... and af - flicted.

8. He was bruised for .... our in - i - qui - ties:
10. And with his .... stripes..... we are healed.

12. We have turned every..... one to his own way.
14. The in - - - iqui - ty of us all. A - men

1st Tenor.

1. Hear! Father, hear our prayer! Thou who art Pity where.. sorrow pre - vaileth,

2d Tenor.

2. Hear! Father, hear our prayer! Wandering unknown in the land of the stranger.
3. Dry thou the mourner's tear; Heal thou the wounds of time hallow'd af - - fection,

1st Bass.

4. Hear! Father, hear our prayer! Long hath thy goodness our footsteps at - tended.

2d Bass.

Thou who art Safety when)
mortal hope faileth, Strength } Hope to des - pair   Hear! Father, hear our prayer.
to the feeble, and........)

Be with all travellers in sick)
ness or danger, Guard thou } feet from the snare. Hear! Father, hear our prayer.
their path, guide their .....)

Grant to the widow and or-)
phan protection, Be in their } friend ever near. Dry thou the mourner's tear.
trouble a ....)

Be with the Pilgrim whose)
journey is ended; When at } death we pre - pare. Hear! Father, hear our prayer. A-men.
thy summons for ....)

1ST TENOR.

1. From the recesses of a lowly spirit, Our humble prayer }
   ascends, O.................................... } Fa - ther,   hear it;
2. We know—we feel how mean, and how unworthy The }
   lowly sacrifice we............................. } pour   be - fore thee;

2D TENOR.

3. Who can resist thy gentle call,—appealing To every }
   generous thought, and.......................... } grate - ful   feeling?—
4. Kind Benefactor!—plant within this bosom The....... seeds of   holiness,—

1ST BASS.

5. Then place them in those everlasting gardens Where }
   angels walk, and............................... } seraphs are the wardens;—

2D BASS.

Borne on the trembling wings of.... fear and meekness; For - give its weakness.
What can we offer thee,—O .... thou most holy! But sin and fol - ly?

O, who can hear the accents .... of thy mercy And   nev - er love thee?
And let them blossom in fragrance, }
and in beauty................... } bright and vernal, And   spring e - ternal.

Where every flower, brought safe }
through....................... } death's dark portal, Be - comes im mortal.

LUKE I. 68—71.

1st TENOR.

1. Blessed be the Lord........................... God of Israel;
2. And hath raised up a mighty sal - - - - - va - tion for us.

2D TENOR.

3. As he spake by the mouth of his.................... ho - ly prophets,
4. That we should be saved........................ from our enemies,

1ST BASS.

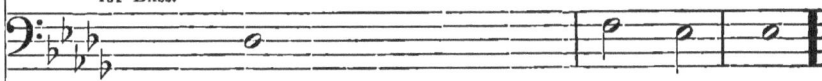

5. Glory be to the Father, and .... to the Son:
6. As it was in the beginning, is now, and............... ever shall be,

2D BASS.

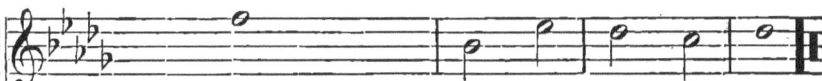

For he hath visited,.................... and re - deemed his people.
In the.................... house of his ser - vant David.

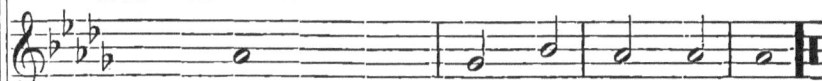

Which have been .... since the world be - gan.
And from the .... hand of all that hate us.

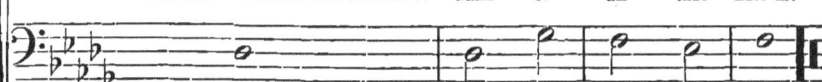

And....................... to the Ho - ly Ghost;
World....................... with - out end A - men.

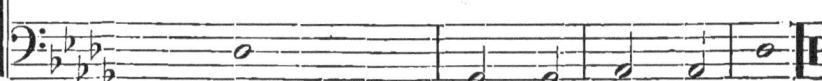

TWENTY-FOURTH OF JUNE.

Words by C. MOORE. [HAVEN. C. M. DOUBLE.] From M. HAYDN.

1ST TENOR.

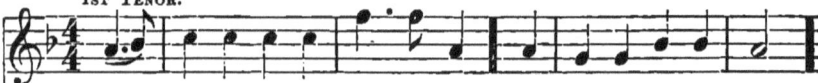

1. All hail! the twen-ty - fourth of June, An - oth - er year has flown;

2D TENOR.

2. On this, an - oth - er fes - tive day, We meet as oft of yore,
3. How sad the thought on memory's page, That some who once were here,

1ST BASS.

4. Then hail the twen-ty - fourth of June! Its memories all are dear,

2D BASS.

And on our al - tar glim - mers yet The Light which long has shone.

And tell of mys-tic la - bors done On mountain vale and shore:
Have no place now but in our hearts—They've reached a high-er sphere:

And oft on fes - tive days like this, Through many a passing year,

Our brethren! ye are wel-come here— A truth-ful no-ble band;

Of fu-ture work we yet may do, Ere we are gathered home,
But Hope points on to fu-ture years, When, all our works com-plete,

We'll meet and grasp each oth-er's hands, Ere yet our work is done;

We're one in mys-tic bonds to-day, We're one in heart and hand.

To hear from our Great Mas-ter's lips, The wel-come words "well done."
The true, and tried, and loved of earth, To-geth-er ALL shall meet.

And, round our al-tars, clo-ser draw The bonds which make us one.

FUNERAL HYMN.

["UNVEIL THY BOSOM, FAITHFUL TOMB."

1st TENOR.

From HANDEL. Arranged for this work.

Unveil thy bosom, faith - ful tomb, Take this new treasure to thy trust, And

p
2D TENOR.

1st BASS.

Unveil thy bosom, faith-ful tomb, Take this new treasure to thy trust, And

2D BASS.

give these sa - cred rel - ics room To slum - ber in the si - lent dust. Nor

give these sa-cred rel - ics room To slum-ber in the si - lent dust. Nor pain, nor grief, nor anxious fear, In-vade thy bounds; no mor-tal woes Can

Cres. Dim.

pain, nor grief, nor anxious fear, In-vade thy bounds; no mor-tal woes Can

Cho. *pp*

reach the si - lent sleep-ers here, And an-gels watch their soft repose. So

Cres - - cen - - do. *f* Dim. Cho. *pp*

reach the si - lent sleep-ers here, And an-gels watch their soft repose, So

Je - sus slept; God's dy - ing Son Passed through the grave, and blessed the bed ; Rest

p

Je - sus slept; God's dy - ing Son Passed through the grave, and blessed the bed ; Rest

here, dear Saint, till from his throne The morn - ing break and pierce the shade.

here, dear Saint, till from his throne The morn - ing break and pierce the shade.

Break from thy throne, il-lus-trious Morn; At - tend, O Earth, his sove - reign word; Re-

Break from thy throne, il-lus-trious Morn; At - tend, O Earth his sove - reign word; Re-

store thy trust, a glo - rious form; Let him ascend to meet his Lord.

store thy trust, a glo - rious form; Let him ascend to meet his Lord.

FUNERAL HYMN.

[PLEYEL'S HYMN. 7s.]

1st Tenor.

1. Sol - emn strikes the funeral chime Notes of our de - part - ing time;

2d Tenor.

2. Mor - tals now in - dulge a tear, For mor - tal - i - ty is here;
3. Here an - oth - er guest we bring; Se - raphs of ce - les - tial wing,

1st Bass.

4. Lord of all, be - low, a - bove, Fill our souls with Truth and Love;

2d Bass.

As we jour - ney here be - low Through a pil - grim - age of wo.

See how wide her tro - phies wave O'er the slum - bers of the grave.
To our funeral al - tar come, Waft our friend and broth - er home.

As dis - solves our earth - ly tie, Take us to thy Lodge on high.

110 FUNERAL HYMN.

1 Wreathe the mourning badge around—
Brothers, pause ! a funeral sound !
Where the parted had his home,
Meet and bear him to the tomb.

2 How his life-path has been trod,
Brothers, leave we unto God !
Friendship's mantle, love and faith,
Lend sweet fragrance e'en to death.

3 Here, amidst the things that sleep,
Let him rest—his grave is deep ;
Death has triumphed, loving hands
Cannot raise him from his bands.

4 Dust to dust, the dark decree—
Soul to God, the soul is free:
Leave him with the lowly slain—
Brothers, we shall meet again.

DEATH OF A BROTHER.

[CHINA. C. M.]

1. What sounds of grief, in sadness, tell A brother's earthly doom, No more in life's fair scenes to dwell, A tenant of the tomb.

2. No more the friendly hand now pressed; No gently-whispered word;
3. All earthly joys and sorrows o'er, Each changing hope or fear;
He finds a long, unbroken rest, Where rules his HEAVENLY LORD.
He sees the light of that fair shore Without a sigh or tear.

4. Then bring to Him, whose only care That better Temple forms, Our wish that all may gather there, Beyond life's coming storms.

107   FUNERAL HYMN.

1 Slowly, in sadness and in tears,
We leave his dwelling now;
It came not once within our fears,
He could so early go.

2 We loved to think of him as one
To whom long years were given;
Who much of good would yet have done,
And late return to heaven.

3 Fair rose his sun of life—few such—
Alas! it set at noon;
His Master must have loved him much,
To call him home so soon.

4 Slowly, in sadness and in tears,
We'll pass his dwelling by;
We mourn the shortness of his years,
And bless his memory.

RESSURRECTION MORN.

[TELEMANN'S CHANT. 7s.]

1ST TENOR.

1. Christ the Lord is risen to - day, Sons of men and an - gels say:

2D TENOR.

1ST BASS.

2. Love's re-deem-ing work is done, Fought the fight, the vic - t'ry won:

2D BASS.

Raise your joys and tri - umphs high, Sing, ye heavens, and earth re - ply.

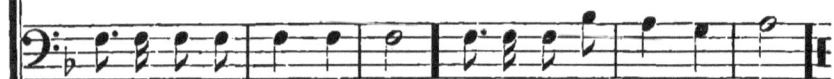

Je - sus' ag - o - ny is o'er, Darkness veils the earth no more.

3 Vain the stone, the watch, the seal,
Christ hath burst the gates of hell ;
Death in vain forbids him rise,
Christ hath opened Paradise

4 Soar we now where Christ hath led,
Following our exalted Head ;
Made like him, like him we rise,
Ours the cross, the grave, the skies.

FUNERAL HYMN.

[MARTYRS. L. M.]　　　　From DONIZETTI.

1st TENOR.

1. With bursting sighs, with notes of woe, What saddening thoughts each bosom swell!

2D TENOR.

2. There sorrowing thoughts and sighs no more O'er death's cold form shall e'er unite;
3. To HIM, our MASTER, humbly bend, Whose Spirit gave our mor - tal breath;

1st BASS.

4. Let Hope's im - mor-tal joys a - rise, Where grief fra-ter-nal fills each breast!

2D BASS.

But Hope directs from scenes be - low To climes where joys im - mor - tal dwell.

No pain shall reach that cloudless shore, Where Love re - flects its ho - ly light.
His hand our stay, when life shall end, Will guide us through the vale of death.

Let Faith di - rect to cloudless skies, Where each shall find his peace-ful rest.

114　　　　FUNERAL HYMN.

1 Here let the sacred rites succeed
In honor of departed friends;
With solemn order now proceed,
While living faith with sorrow blends.

2 Now let the hymn—the humble prayer,
From hearts sincere, ascend on high,
And mystic evergreen declare
That Hope within us cannot die.

3 The mortal frame may be concealed
Within the narrow house of gloom;
But God, in mercy, has revealed
Immortal life beyond the tomb.

4 The friends we mourn we still may love;
Then let our aspirations rise
To that bright spirit-world above,
Where virtue lives, love never dies.

FUNERAL HYMN.

GERMAN.

1ST TENOR.

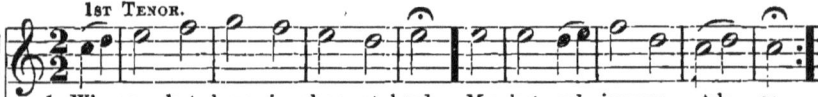

1. When my last hour is close at hand, My last sad journey tak - en,
   Do Thou, Lord Je - sus! by me stand; Let me not be for - sak - en.

2D TENOR.

2. Count-less as sands up - on the shore, My sins may then ap - pall me;
   Yet, though my conscience vex me sore, De-spair shall not en - thrall me;

3. I shall not in the grave re - main, Since Thou death's bonds hast sev-ered;
   By Hope with Thee to rise a - gain, From fear of death de - liv - ered.

1ST BASS.

4. And so to Je - sus Christ I'll go, My long-ing arms ex - tend - ing;
   So fall a - sleep in slum-ber deep, Slumber that knows no wak - ing;

2D BASS.

O Lord! my spir - it I re - sign In - to thy lov - ing

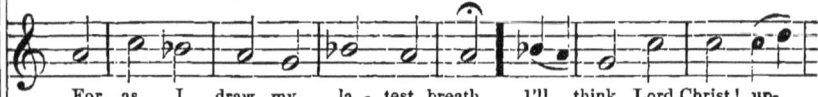

For as I draw my la - test breath, I'll think, Lord Christ! up-
I'll come to Thee, wher - e'er Thou art, Live with Thee, from Thee

Till Je - sus Christ, God's on - ly Son, Op - ens the gates of

hands di - vine; 'Tis safe with - in thy keep - ing.

on thy death, And there find con - so - la - tion.
nev - er part; There - fore I die in rap - ture.

bliss, leads on, To Heaven, to life e - ter - nal,

---

116 TEMPLAR'S FUNERAL.

(Music on page 57. c. m.)

1 What means this pageantry of Knights,—
This gath'ring here to-day ?
Why are these weeping ones thus clad
In sorrow's dark array ?

2 A Christian warrior here has fall'n,—
Has laid his armor by ;
Has reached th' asylum of the blest,
A mansion in the sky.

3 With faith in immortality,
With hope e'er beaming bright,
A knightly soldier of the cross
Has fought the Christian fight.

4 Then look not on that lifeless form,
Nor seek him here below ;
By faith behold him on that shore
Where life's pure waters flow.

H. G. BARROWS

---

117 DEATH OF A BROTHER.

(Music on page 57. c. m.)

1 As, bowed by sudden storms, the rose
Sinks on the garden's breast,
Down to the grave our brother goes,
In silence there to rest.

2 No more with us his tuneful voice
The mystic hymn shall swell ;
No more his cheerful heart rejoice
When peals the Sabbath bell.

3 But far away, in cloudless sphere,
Amid a sinless throng,
He's joining, with celestial ear,
The everlasting song.

4 No more we'll mourn our absent friend,
But lift our earnest prayer,
That when our work of life shall end
We all may join him there.

DEAD MARCH FROM "SAUL."

HANDEL.

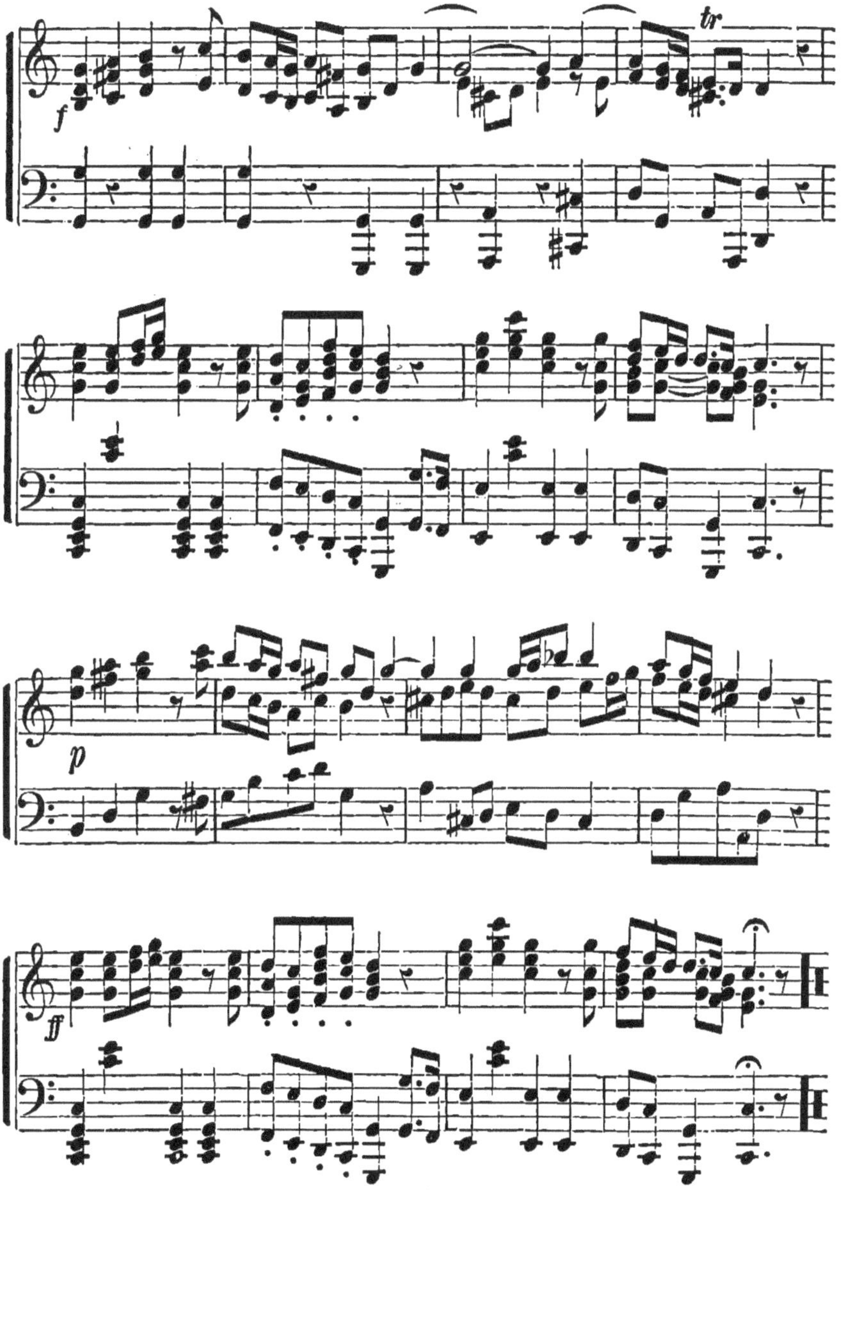
tr
f
p
ff

SLOW MARCH.

From BEETHOVEN.

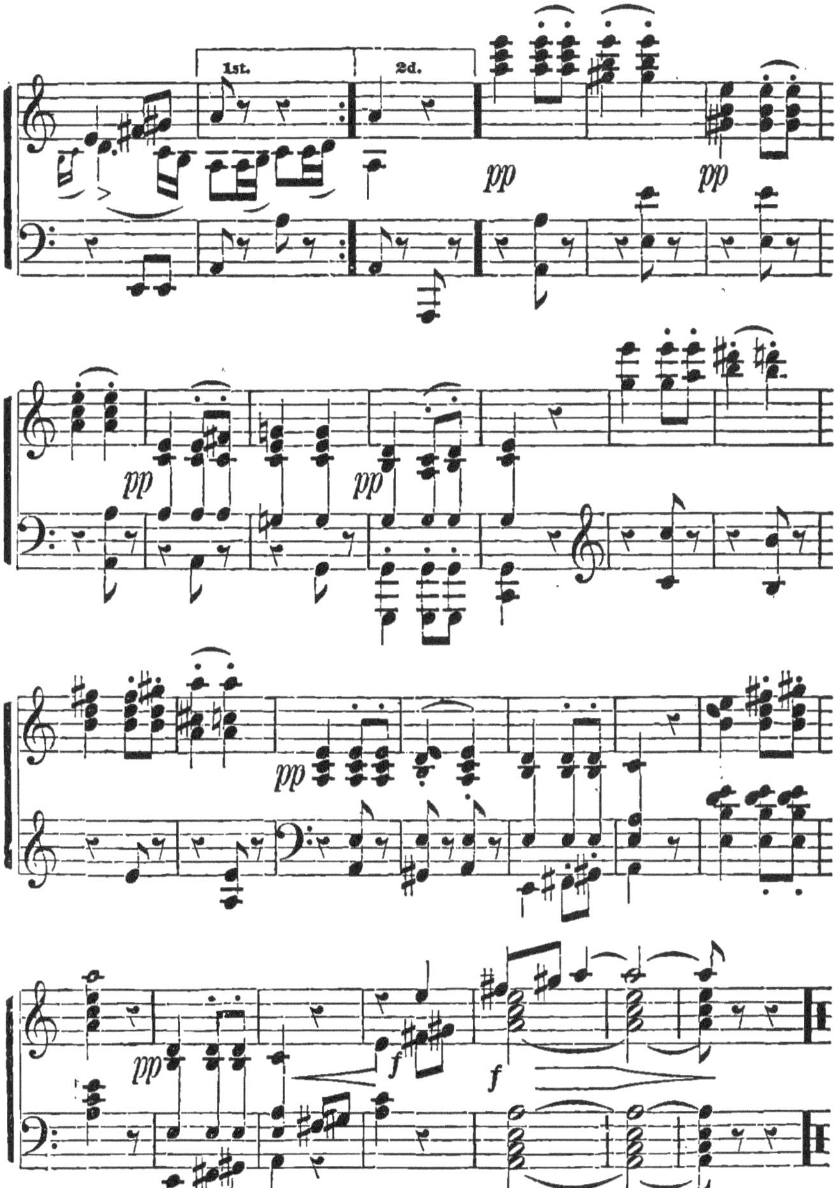
1st.
2d.
pp
pp
pp
pp
pp
pp
f
f

MARCH RELIGIOSO.

Marziale. M.M. ♩ = 86.

From Costa's "Eli."

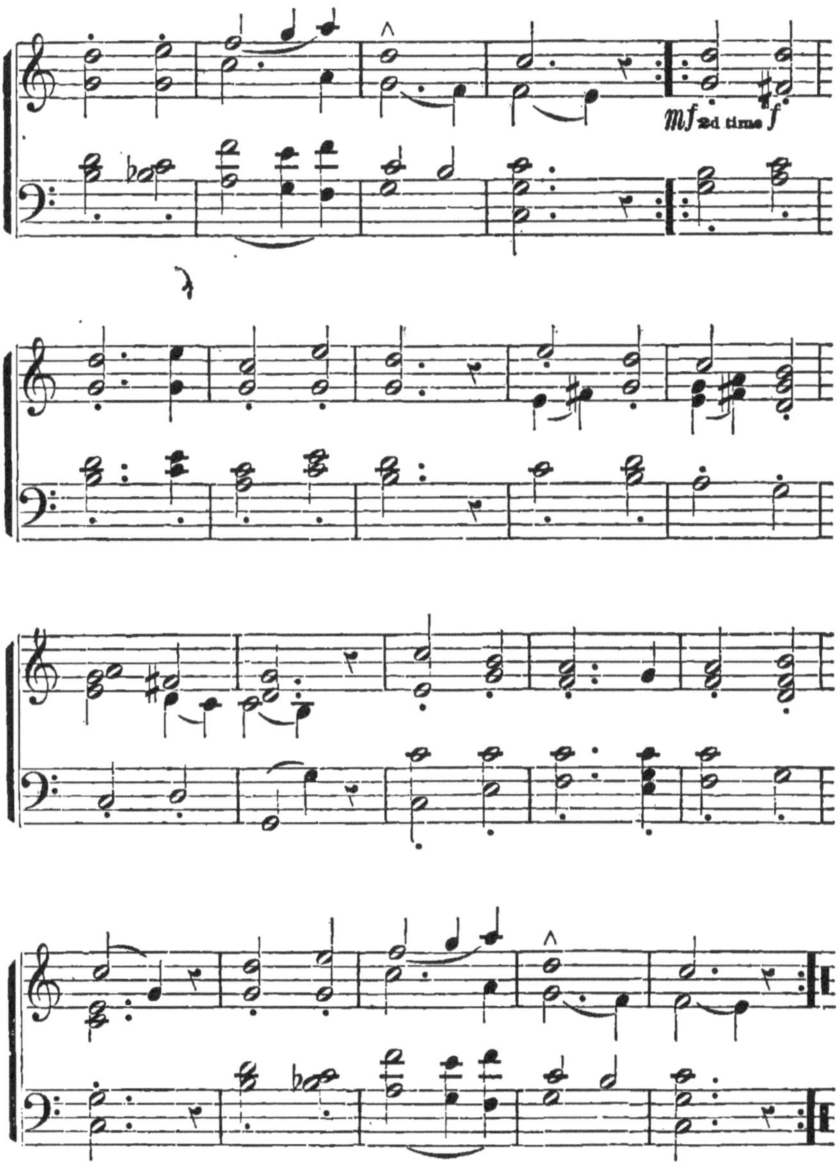
mf 2d time f

MARCH MILITAIRE.

S. WESLEY.

With dignity.

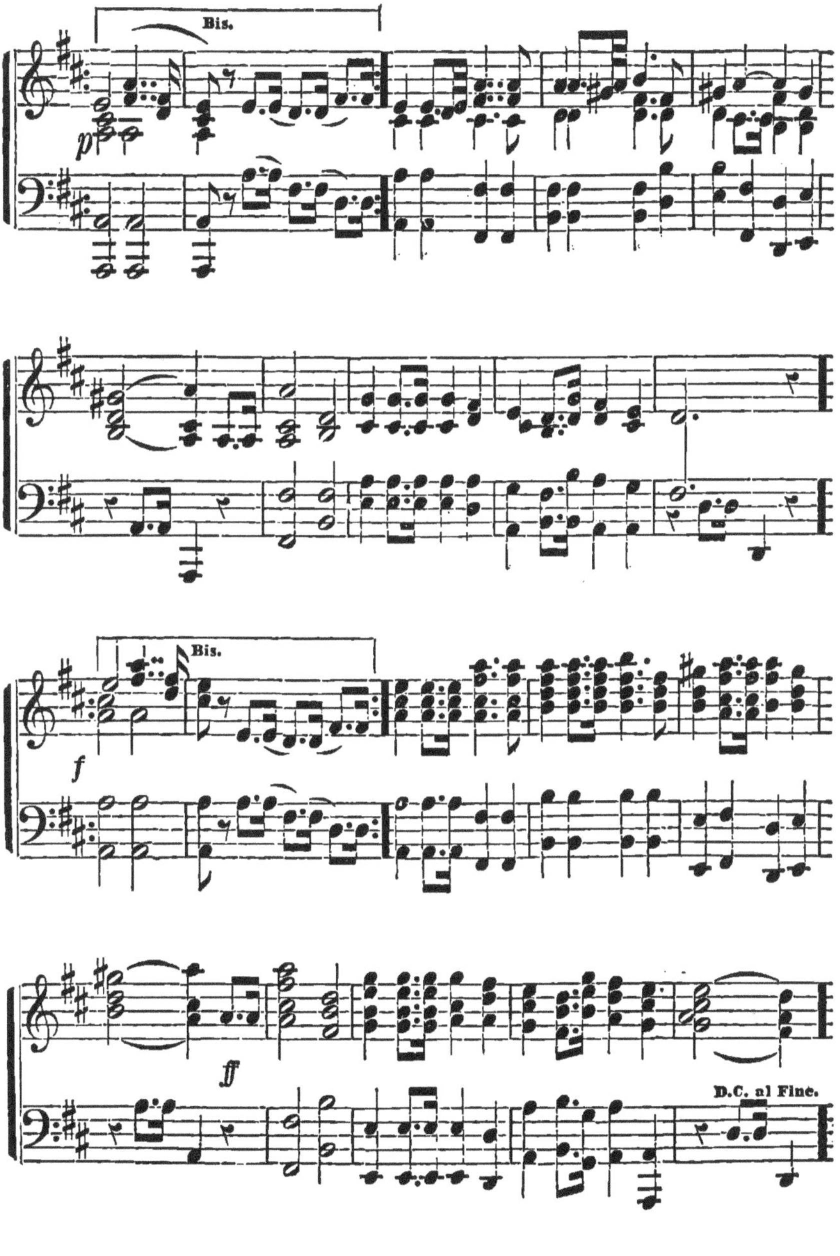
Bis.
p
Bis.
f
ff
D.C. al Fine.

THE CHRISTIAN WARRIORS.

[WILMOT. 8s & 7s.]

1ST TENOR.

1. Chris-tian war-riors, to the peal-ing Of the sol-emn ves-per bell,

2D TENOR.

1ST BASS.

2. When the watch and ward are o-ver, Guarding the A-sy-lum well,

2D BASS.

Round the tri-form al-tar kneeling, Whisper each, E-man-u-el.

Smiles of Peace a-round them hov-er, At thy name, E-man-u-el.

3 When the matin-notes are ringing
  Cheerfully from mount and dell,
Strength for warfare still is springing
From thy name, Emanuel.

4 When some deed of empire sharing,
  Deeds like those traditions tell
Prompts each Knight to noble daring,
'Tis for Thee, Emanuel.

5 When the storm-clouds darkly lower
  On our pathway dark and fell,
Knights heroic will not cower,
  Cheered by Thee, Emanuel.

6 When death's fearful damps are stealing,
  And is breathed the last "Farewell!"
All the brighter world revealing,
  Thou shalt come, Emanuel.

INDEX OF SUBJECTS.

Part I. Blue Lodge.

Part II. Chapter.

Part III. Encampment.

Part IV. Council of Royal and Select Masters.

Part V. Miscellaneous.

INDEX OF TUNES.